323
H887

AUG 2012

CH

INTRODUCING
ISSUES WITH
OPPOSING
VIEWPOINTS®

Human Rights

Lauri S. Friedman, *Book Editor*

GREENHAVEN PRESS
A part of Gale, Cengage Learning

GALE
CENGAGE Learning™

Detroit • New York • San Francisco • New Haven, Conn • Waterville, Maine • London

GALE
CENGAGE Learning

Christine Nasso, *Publisher*
Elizabeth Des Chenes, *Managing Editor*

For more information, contact:
Greenhaven Press
27500 Drake Rd.
Farmington Hills, MI 48331-3535
Or you can visit our Internet site at gale.cengage.com

Articles in Greenhaven Press anthologies are often edited for length to meet page requirements. In addition, original titles of these works are changed to clearly present the main thesis and to explicitly indicate the author's opinion. Every effort is made to ensure that Greenhaven Press accurately reflects the original intent of the authors. Every effort has been made to trace the owners of copyrighted material.

Cover image © Mark Peterson/Documentary/Corbis

LIBRARY OF CONGRESS CATALOGING-IN-PUBLICATION DATA

Human rights / Lauri S. Friedman, book editor.
   p. cm. -- (Introducing issues with opposing viewpoints)
Includes bibliographical references and index.
ISBN 978-0-7377-4478-1 (hardcover)
1. Human rights 2. Human rights--United States. I. Friedman, Lauri S.
JC571.H76845 2010
323--dc22

2009033681

Printed in the United States of America
2 3 4 5 6 7 13 12 11 10

Contents

Chapter 3: What Human Rights Policies Should the United States Follow?

Foreword

Indulging in a wide spectrum of ideas, beliefs, and perspectives is a critical cornerstone of democracy. After all, it is often debates over differences of opinion, such as whether to legalize abortion, how to treat prisoners, or when to enact the death penalty, that shape our society and drive it forward. Such diversity of thought is frequently regarded as the hallmark of a healthy and civilized culture. As the Reverend Clifford Schutjer of the First Congregational Church in Mansfield, Ohio, declared in a 2001 sermon, "Surrounding oneself with only like-minded people, restricting what we listen to or read only to what we find agreeable is irresponsible. Refusing to entertain doubts once we make up our minds is a subtle but deadly form of arrogance." With this advice in mind, Introducing Issues with Opposing Viewpoints books aim to open readers' minds to the critically divergent views that comprise our world's most important debates.

Introducing Issues with Opposing Viewpoints simplifies for students the enormous and often overwhelming mass of material now available via print and electronic media. Collected in every volume is an array of opinions that captures the essence of a particular controversy or topic. Introducing Issues with Opposing Viewpoints books embody the spirit of nineteenth-century journalist Charles A. Dana's axiom: "Fight for your opinions, but do not believe that they contain the whole truth, or the only truth." Absorbing such contrasting opinions teaches students to analyze the strength of an argument and compare it to its opposition. From this process readers can inform and strengthen their own opinions, or be exposed to new information that will change their minds. Introducing Issues with Opposing Viewpoints is a mosaic of different voices. The authors are statesmen, pundits, academics, journalists, corporations, and ordinary people who have felt compelled to share their experiences and ideas in a public forum. Their words have been collected from newspapers, journals, books, speeches, interviews, and the Internet, the fastest growing body of opinionated material in the world.

Introducing Issues with Opposing Viewpoints shares many of the well-known features of its critically acclaimed parent series, Opposing Viewpoints. The articles are presented in a pro/con format, allowing readers to absorb divergent perspectives side by side. Active reading questions preface each viewpoint, requiring the student to approach the material thoughtfully and carefully. Useful charts, graphs, and cartoons supplement each article. A thorough introduction provides readers with crucial background on an issue. An annotated bibliography points the reader toward articles, books, and Web sites that contain additional information on the topic. An appendix of organizations to contact contains a wide variety of charities, nonprofit organizations, political groups, and private enterprises that each hold a position on the issue at hand. Finally, a comprehensive index allows readers to locate content quickly and efficiently.

Introducing Issues with Opposing Viewpoints is also significantly different from Opposing Viewpoints. As the series title implies, its presentation will help introduce students to the concept of opposing viewpoints and learn to use this material to aid in critical writing and debate. The series' four-color, accessible format makes the books attractive and inviting to readers of all levels. In addition, each viewpoint has been carefully edited to maximize a reader's understanding of the content. Short but thorough viewpoints capture the essence of an argument. A substantial, thought-provoking essay question placed at the end of each viewpoint asks the student to further investigate the issues raised in the viewpoint, compare and contrast two authors' arguments, or consider how one might go about forming an opinion on the topic at hand. Each viewpoint contains sidebars that include at-a-glance information and handy statistics. A Facts About section located in the back of the book further supplies students with relevant facts and figures.

Following in the tradition of the Opposing Viewpoints series, Greenhaven Press continues to provide readers with invaluable exposure to the controversial issues that shape our world. As John Stuart Mill once wrote: "The only way in which a human being can make some approach to knowing the whole of a subject is by hearing what can be said about it by persons of every variety of opinion and studying all modes in which it can be looked at by every character of mind. No wise man ever acquired his wisdom in any mode but this." It is to this principle that Introducing Issues with Opposing Viewpoints books are dedicated.

Introduction

America established its reputation as a beacon of human rights early in its history. This reputation was solidified as it became embroiled in the Cold War, a multi-decade conflict with the communist Soviet Union for power and influence around the globe. In the ideological standoff between the two superpowers, the United States represented democracy, freedom, opportunity, and hope, which was attractive to citizens of almost every country on earth.

But since that time, the United States has faced new enemies and dealt with them in ways that have brought much controversy on itself. In the war on terror—which officially began following the terrorist attacks of September 11, 2001, in which nearly three thousand Americans were killed—the United States embarked on a terrorist-catching mission that caused it to use tactics that some have described as torture.

As early as 2002, George W. Bush administration officials approved the use of harsh interrogation tactics to debrief suspected enemies about potential terrorist plans. The most famous of these techniques is waterboarding, a process in which interrogators make a suspect feel as though he is drowning by restraining him and either dunking him in water or pouring water over his face. During the practice, a person is strapped faceup to a long board and tilted at an angle, so his head is lower than his heart. Then, his legs and arms are restrained to the board while his head is covered with a hood and several towels. Finally water is poured over his head, invoking the sensation of drowning and causing him to inhale water.

Interestingly, waterboarding used to be something that American soldiers were trained to resist, rather than inflict on others. In fact, many American soldiers experienced waterboarding as part of a high-level training program known as Survival, Evasion, Resistance, and Escape (SERE). This program taught them how to resist forms of torture so they would know what to do if they were ever captured by enemy troops who might practice it. But as the United States faced terrorists who would stop at nothing to kill innocent Americans—

people who would even sacrifice their own lives if it meant being able to kill others—it seemed that new measures were needed for the United States to triumph. And so waterboarding and other previously unused methods made their way onto the approved list of U.S. interrogation tactics.

Christopher Hitchens, a writer for *Vanity Fair*, was voluntarily waterboarded by veteran U.S. soldiers in 2008 to evaluate whether or not the technique should be counted as torture. He reports on the experience:

> In this pregnant darkness, head downward, I waited for a while until I abruptly felt a slow cascade of water going up my nose. Determined to resist . . . , I held my breath for a while and then had to exhale and—as you might expect—inhale in turn. The inhalation brought the damp cloths tight against my nostrils, as if a huge, wet paw had been suddenly and annihilatingly clamped over my face.[1]

Although he had wanted to see if he could endure the procedure for at least ninety seconds (the time it took terrorist Khalid Sheik Mohammad, the mastermind behind the September 11 terrorist attacks, to crack under the technique), Hitchens was unable to take it for more than a couple. "Unable to determine whether I was breathing in or out, and flooded more with sheer panic than with mere water, I triggered the pre-arranged signal and felt the unbelievable relief of being pulled upright and having the soaking and stifling layers pulled off me."[2]

Hitchens's personal experience led him to conclude that waterboarding is indeed a form of torture, and the United States should not be doing it—but not all of America is in complete agreement with him. It is true that many Americans regard waterboarding as torture: A 2009 Ipsos/McClatchy poll found that 60 percent of Americans consider waterboarding as such, and even more answered this way when surveyed in a CBS News/*New York Times* poll, which found 71 percent of Americans consider waterboarding to be torture. Yet many believe suspected terrorists should be tortured if it will help interrupt their plans to kill innocent Americans: An April 2009 Gallup Poll found that 55 percent of Americans believe it is justified to use harsh interrogation tactics such as waterboarding to extract information from suspected terrorists.

Typically, controversy over whether torture should be used on terrorist suspects focuses less on whether it is right or wrong and more on whether it is effective. In some cases the use of waterboarding on a suspected terrorist has revealed valuable information. For example, waterboarding Khalid Sheik Mohammad for less than two minutes resulted in his telling authorities information that led to the identification and arrest of six other terrorists. For this reason, Deroy Murdock, a supporter of waterboarding, says, "Though clearly uncomfortable, waterboarding loosens lips without causing permanent physical injuries (and unlikely even temporary ones). If terrorists suffer long-term nightmares about waterboarding, better that than more Americans crying themselves to sleep after their loved ones have been shredded by bombs or baked in skyscrapers."[3] In Murdock's opinion, waterboarding is something every American should be proud of because it shows powerful resolve to protect their country.

Yet others are suspect of information that is revealed during an interrogation that involves torture. Too often, it is said, the person being interrogated will lie or make false confessions just to make the torture stop. Information obtained under such circumstances is untrustworthy, as one former FBI officer testified before the Senate in 2009. "Such techniques, from an operational perspective, are ineffective, slow and unreliable, and harmful to our efforts to defeat al Qaeda,"[4] said Ali Soufan, who served as an FBI special agent from 1997 to 2005. "I saw that using these alternative methods on other terrorists backfired on more than a few occasions—all of which are still classified. The short sightedness behind the use of these techniques ignored the unreliability of the methods."[5]

Also open to debate is the issue of whether the United States should be in the business of using torture to interrogate suspects at all. Some believe it is the right approach for dealing with a new, particularly insidious enemy; others believe it corrodes the positive image of America that was built throughout the twentieth century. Whether the United States does or should use torture to interrogate suspected terrorists is just one of the issues explored in *Introducing Issues with Opposing Viewpoints: Human Rights*. In addition to considering what human rights policies the United States should follow, readers will also ponder what constitutes a human rights violation and where human rights are most abused. Readers will examine these issues in article pairs, and thought-provoking essay questions will help them form their own opinions on the topic.

Notes

1. Christopher Hitchens, "Believe Me, It's Torture," *Vanity Fair*, August 2008.

2. Hitchens, "Believe Me, It's Torture."

3. Deroy Murdock, "Waterboarding Has Its Benefits: Tortured 'Repugnant' Arguments," *National Review*, November 5, 2007.

4. Quoted in Pam Benson, "'Enhanced Interrogations' Don't Work, Ex-FBI Agent Tells Panel," CNN.com, May 13, 2009. www.edition .cnn.com/2009/POLITICS/05/13/interrogation.hearing/index.html.

5. Ali Soufan, "My Tortured Decision," *New York Times*, April 22, 2009.

Chapter 1

What Are Some Human Rights?

On June 4, 2009, thousands of people in Hong Kong attend a candlelight vigil to mark the twentieth anniversary of the Chinese government's crackdown on human rights protestors in Tiananmen Square in Beijing on June 4, 1989.

Health Care Is a Human Right

Benjamin Danielson and Hugh Foy

"State and federal lawmakers . . . should treat health care not as just another consumer product, but as a basic human right."

In the following viewpoint Benjamin Danielson and Hugh Foy argue that health care should be treated as a human right. They explain that when people are sick and do not have health insurance, their illnesses tend to get worse because they do not seek care for financial reasons. So, when they are finally treated, their condition costs more to fix. Danielson and Foy argue that these costs are passed on to every American in other forms. But beyond finances, Danielson and Foy think it is immoral to let people suffer by putting health care out of their reach. They conclude that human rights principles should drive efforts to create health care coverage for everyone.

Danielson is medical director of the Odessa Brown Children's Clinic and teaches at the University of Washington. Foy is a physician, surgeon, and educator who practices in Seattle, Washington.

AS YOU READ, CONSIDER THE FOLLOWING QUESTIONS:
1. Who are Joey and David, and how do they factor into the authors' argument?

Benjamin Danielson and Hugh Foy, "Treat Health Care as a Human Right," *Post-Intelligencer* (Seattle), January 28, 2009. Reproduced by permission of the authors.

2. What do the authors say that the Northwest Health Law Advocates found about health care reform proposals?
3. What, according to Danielson and Foy, did more than one thousand people in Washington State emphasize the need for in 2008?

With our economy in crisis, President Barack Obama newly sworn in and health reform hearings under way [in January 2009] in the Legislature, only one thing is certain about U.S. health care: We cannot afford the status quo.

The silver lining in this crisis is that it offers us the opportunity to build a high-quality, sustainable health system—one founded on the premise that every person should be able to get the health care they need, rather than viewing health care as a consumer product that we can buy or forgo.

The Uninsured Pass Costs on to All of Us

Patients get sicker, and cost more, when care is delayed. Take, for example, Joey, an uninsured 3-year-old whose mother couldn't afford asthma medications. As a result, Joey wound up in the emergency room with a serious asthma flare costing 10 to 15 times more than the medicine that would have prevented it. Or David, a retired store manager who, despite his Medicare coverage, was unable to find a doctor to treat complications of stepping on a thumbtack with a foot rendered numb from years of diabetes, because he lacked a Medicare supplemental policy. After searching for weeks in vain, he finally came to the hospital, his foot now afflicted with

FAST FACT

According to the Public Broadcasting Service, fewer and fewer Americans get health insurance at their job: Employment-based health coverage has dropped nearly 10 percent over the past twenty years.

gangrene and in need of an emergency amputation. Timely care would have saved his foot at a tiny fraction of the cost.

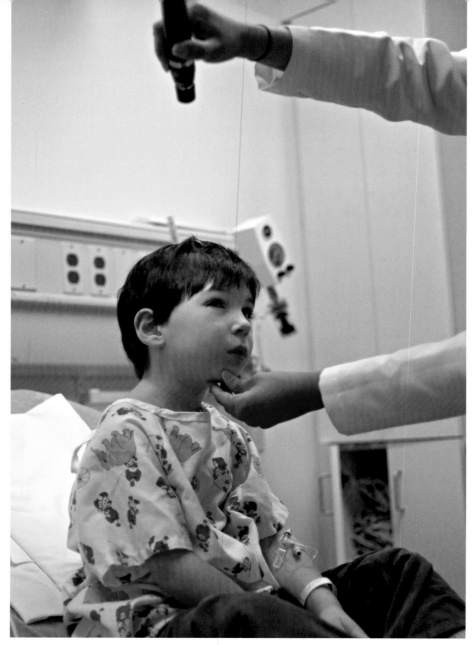

A parent who cannot afford the cost of medication or preventive treatment for an uninsured child will incur far greater costs if the child requires an emergency room visit, the authors argue.

As a society, we pay dearly, in human terms and in cold dollars, when people lack access to care. Now, with such giants as Microsoft, Starbucks, Boeing and Washington Mutual announcing job layoffs, more people will lose their health benefits. And, like Joey and David, when they get sick or injured, many will get care only when their situation becomes an emergency. Those high expenses are passed on to all of us in the form of skyrocketing health costs.

In an effort to develop options, the Legislature commissioned an economic analysis of five state health reform proposals. The analysis, prepared by Mathematica Policy Research, will be presented at hearings this week. In these tumultuous times, it may be tempting for lawmakers to favor the plan that costs the least in the short run, or to take no action. But that won't make people's unmet health needs go away.

As physicians, we believe the only way to create a durable system—one that is equitable and affordable, allowing everyone to get the care they need—is to design it around human rights principles that make protection of health paramount.

Using that approach, Northwest Health Law Advocates [NoHLA] has just released a human rights evaluation of the five proposals that complements Mathematica's primarily economic analysis (available at nohla.org). NoHLA found that some reform proposals—those that would cover all state residents—are better than others but all need to pay more attention to human rights values.

We Owe Health Care to Our Fellow Citizens

And that is what [Americans] want. In eight health care caucuses around the state [of Washington] in 2008, more than 1,000 people emphasized the need for universal coverage, affordability and access for all, reflecting those values.

Fortunately, the ethical choice is also the economically prudent choice. There is a false perception that we must choose between lower cost and broader access.

But creating a health system for all is the only sustainable solution over the long haul. It is the only way to prevent the sad stories and poor health outcomes physicians see every day. The quick fixes will just widen disparities and reduce access, which will drive up costs in the long run. Investing in comprehensive coverage, so the Joeys and Davids of our country get timely, appropriate care rather than requiring expensive treatment, will save money and improve health.

Who Are the Uninsured in America?

Nearly 45 million people are uninsured in America. Almost 70 percent of them come from a family with at least one full-time worker.

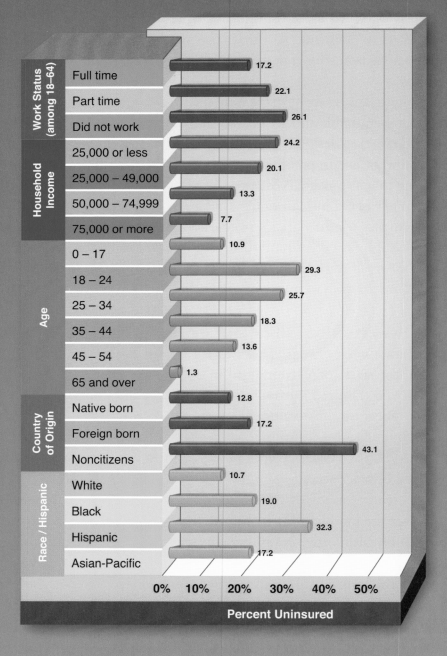

Work Status (among 18–64)
- Full time: 17.2
- Part time: 22.1
- Did not work: 26.1

Household Income
- 25,000 or less: 24.2
- 25,000 – 49,000: 20.1
- 50,000 – 74,999: 13.3
- 75,000 or more: 7.7

Age
- 0 – 17: 10.9
- 18 – 24: 29.3
- 25 – 34: 25.7
- 35 – 44: 18.3
- 45 – 54: 13.6
- 65 and over: 1.3

Country of Origin
- Native born: 12.8
- Foreign born: 17.2
- Noncitizens: 43.1

Race / Hispanic
- White: 10.7
- Black: 19.0
- Hispanic: 32.3
- Asian-Pacific: 17.2

Percent Uninsured

Taken from: U.S. Census Bureau, Current Population Survey, 2006 Annual Social and Economic Supplement.

The best measure of who we are as a people is how we behave in times of crisis. As state and federal lawmakers consider options for reform, they should treat health care not as just another consumer product, but as a basic human right, like clean air and water.

EVALUATING THE AUTHORS' ARGUMENTS:

Benjamin Danielson and Hugh Foy are both doctors. Do you think this background increases the credibility of their argument? Explain why or why not.

Viewpoint

2

Health Care Is Not a Human Right

Donald J. Boudreaux

"Only by abandoning attempts to provide healthcare as a 'right' that's paid for largely by others will we enjoy surer access to it."

Health care should not be regarded as a human right, Donald J. Boudreaux argues in the following viewpoint. He claims that free, universal health care would ultimately hurt more Americans than currently suffer from being uninsured. If health care were free to all, Boudreaux thinks its quality would decline. He also thinks services would be overaccessed—people would seek medical care unnecessarily, which would drain the system and cost millions. Furthermore, it would not *really* be free—someone would have to pay for it, and Boudreaux argues that it would be the taxpayers. Ultimately, he predicts the government would have to tightly ration health care to make sure everyone received it equally. For these reasons, Boudreaux argues health care should not be treated like a human right but as a service or product people have to pay for.

Boudreaux is chair of the economics department at George Mason University.

Donald J. Boudreaux, "The Way to Better, Cheaper Healthcare: Don't Make It a Human Right," *Christian Science Monitor,* October 17, 2006. Reproduced by permission of the author.

AS YOU READ, CONSIDER THE FOLLOWING QUESTIONS:
  1. What, according to Boudreaux, constitutes a right?
  2. Why does the author think making a service like food or health care free would lead to government rationing?
  3. Why does the author think it is hard to say what constitutes "essential care"?

E veryone complains about the rising cost of healthcare. And now is the season when politicians and pundits propose solutions. Unfortunately, too many of these proposals spring from the wrongheaded notion that healthcare is, as a recent *New York Times* letter-writer asserted, "a human right and a universal entitlement."

Sounds noble. But not everything that is highly desirable is a right. Most rights simply oblige us to respect one another's freedoms; they do not oblige us to pay for others to exercise these freedoms. Respecting rights such as freedom of speech and of worship does not impose huge demands upon taxpayers.

Healthcare Is Not a "Right"

Healthcare, although highly desirable, differs fundamentally from these rights. Because providing healthcare takes scarce resources, offering it free at the point of delivery would raise its cost and reduce its availability.

To see why, imagine if government tried to supply food as a universally available "right."

To satisfy this right, government would raise taxes to meet all anticipated food needs. Store shelves across the land would then be stocked. Citizens would have the right to enter these storehouses to get "free" food.

> **FAST FACT**
>
> According to the World Health Organization, the United States spends more than 15 percent of its gross domestic product on health care, a greater portion than any other United Nations member state except for the Marshall Islands.

Does anyone believe that such a system would effectively supply food? It's clear that with free access to food, too many people would take too much food, leaving many others with no food at all. Government would soon realize that food storehouses are emptying faster than expected. In response, it might hike taxes even higher to produce more food—raising the price that society pays for nutrition.

Stocking stores with more food, though, won't solve the problem. With food free at the point of delivery, consumers would take all that they can carry. People would quickly learn that if they don't grab as much food as possible today, the store might run out of the foods that their families need tomorrow. This creates a vicious cycle of moral hazard that unwittingly pits neighbor against neighbor.

Eventually, to avoid spending impossibly large chunks of society's resources producing food, government would start restricting access to it. Bureaucrats would enforce rations, such as "two gallons of milk per family per week." There might be exceptions for those with special needs, but most of us would be allowed to take only those foods that officials decide we need.

The author contends that government-run health care would be comparable to the government's running free grocery stores for which taxpayers would foot the bill.

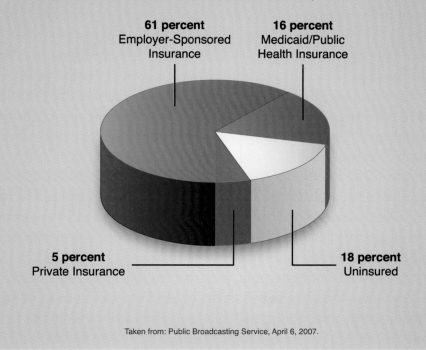

Most Americans Are Already Insured

The majority of Americans are insured, either through their employer, through public insurance like Medicaid, or privately.

61 percent
Employer-Sponsored
Insurance

16 percent
Medicaid/Public
Health Insurance

5 percent
Private Insurance

18 percent
Uninsured

Taken from: Public Broadcasting Service, April 6, 2007.

Food would be a universal entitlement in name only. In practice, it would be strictly limited by government rules. Of course, by keeping what food it does supply "free," government might ensure that at least basic foodstuffs are available to everyone as a right. And maybe this is the sort of outcome that universal healthcare advocates have in mind: Only essential care is a right to be enjoyed by everyone free of charge.

Where to Draw the Line at "Essential"

The problem is that notions of "essential care" are vague. Is medical care essential if doctors say it might improve by 50 percent an 80-year-old's chances of living an additional year? What about care that improves by 10 percent a 25-year-old's chances of living an additional 50 years? Such questions are wickedly difficult to answer.

Despite these difficulties, many Americans demand that government do more to guarantee access to healthcare. Although their concern is understandable, those who make such demands forget that government intervention itself is a major cause of today's high and rising healthcare costs. Indeed, this intervention has created a situation akin to what would happen if government supplied our food for "free."

Medicare, Medicaid, and tax-deductibility of employer-provided health insurance created a system in which patients at the point of delivery now pay only a small fraction of their medical bills out of pocket. This situation leads to monstrously inefficient consumption of healthcare. Some people consume too much, while many others with more pressing needs do without.

Because the wasteful consumption caused by heavily subsidized access drives up healthcare costs, taxpayers must pay more and more to fund Medicare and Medicaid, while private insurers must continually raise premiums. The sad and perverse result is that increasing numbers of people go without health insurance.

The solution is less, not more, government involvement in healthcare. Market forces have consistently lowered the cost and improved the quality and accessibility of food—which is at least as important to human survival as is healthcare. There's no reason markets can't do the same for healthcare.

It's ironic but true: Only by abandoning attempts to provide healthcare as a "right" that's paid by others will we enjoy surer access to it.

EVALUATING THE AUTHOR'S ARGUMENTS:

Boudreaux uses the hypothetical example of "free" food to frame his argument that health care should not be treated as a right. In your opinion, is it appropriate to compare food with health care? Why or why not?

Access to Clean Water Is a Human Right

Maude Barlow

"People have the right to demand safe, clean drinking water publicly delivered by their governments on a not-for-profit basis as a basic human right."

In the following viewpoint Maude Barlow argues that access to clean, free water should be regarded as a human right. Because everyone needs water to live, Barlow says it is no different from air, for which a fee would never be charged. She classifies water not as a "want" but as a "need." As such, she says, companies should not be allowed to profit from something as vital as access to water. When water delivery is privatized for profit, the author says, it costs more, reaches fewer people, is of poorer quality, and causes job loss. Barlow concludes it is the responsibility of governments, not of for-profit companies, to make sure that citizens have free access to clean water.

Barlow is the senior adviser on water to the president of the United Nations General Assembly. She is also the author of *Blue Covenant: The Global Water Crisis and the Coming Battle for the Right to Water.*

Maude Barlow, "Water Is a Human Right," *San Francisco Chronicle,* January 22, 2009. Reproduced by permission of the author.

AS YOU READ, CONSIDER THE FOLLOWING QUESTIONS:
1. What does the author say private water companies have to do with their profits?
2. Name at least two ways in which Barlow suggests private water companies can help bring water to all people.
3. What would corporate control of water discourage, according to Barlow?

I n a world running out of clean, accessible water, the question of who decides its allocation is crucial. Is access to water a human right or just a need? Is water a common good like air or a commodity like Coca-Cola? Who is being given the right or the power to turn on or off the tap—the people, governments or the invisible hand of the market? Who sets the price of water for a poor district in Manila [the Philippines] or La Paz [Mexico]—the locally elected water board or the CEO [chief executive officer] of a big water corporation?

This is an important and controversial issue. A U.N. [United Nations] covenant would put nation-states on notice that it is their responsibility to provide clean water to their citizens. People have the right to demand safe, clean drinking water publicly delivered by their governments on a not-for-profit basis as a basic human right. The World Bank and the United Nations must make it a priority to build and support robust public institutions that guarantee water for all.

FAST FACT

According to the Pacific Institute, more than 1 billion people lack access to safe drinking water, and 2.5 billion people live without access to adequate sanitation systems necessary to reduce exposure to water-related diseases.

Privatized Water Does Not Work

I have studied the history of for-profit water delivery in the Southern Hemisphere, which was imposed by the World Bank as a condition of funding, and the record is clear: Privatized water delivery results in high water rates, worker layoffs, decreased services, reduced water quality and water cutoffs to untold millions. Even the best private water companies must cut corners and use profits to pay dividends to their investors rather than investing in improved facilities.

Perhaps the greatest indictment of commercializing water delivery is the fact that, anticipating that the private sector would bring new investments for water services in poor countries, the lending banks and wealthy country donor agencies decreased their funding for water projects between 1998 and 2002—a time when the need for services and aid in the global South exponentially grew.

This is not to say that there have not been public sector failures to provide clean water. There have. But governments are accountable to their citizens and can be changed.

Nor is this to suggest there is no place for the private sector in helping to find solutions to the global water crisis. Business has an important role in laying pipes, building infrastructure and cleaning and recycling dirty water. There is a huge role for the private sector

People fill water cans at a distribution site in Kenya. The author warns that clean, safe drinking water is becoming increasingly scarce, especially in developing countries such as Kenya.

People Need Water to Live

Water is not a luxury—everyone needs it to survive. According to the United Nations, the planet is due for a catastrophic water shortage that will claim many lives.

1970 – Warning Signs

In 1970 water consumption worldwide was half what it is today. With 80% of all sickness in the developing world linked to polluted water, and with populations sharply on the rise, the urgency of water management became apparent.

2003 – Dry and Dirty

Over 1.3 billion people have no access to clean water. At least 2.2 million people die annually from diseases related to poor sanitation and contaminated drinking water—that is about 10,000 deaths from bad water (or no water) each day.

2025 – Parched Populace

The United Nations estimates that the world's per capita water supply will drop by one-third in the next 20 years. The worst strain will be in Africa and the Middle East, where populations are growing fast and rivers are running dry.

Who will have the water?

Percentage of world water supply by natural economic region

>20	10-20	5-10	2-5	1-2	<1

Taken from: United Nations, *Montreal Gazette*, Unesco, *New York Times*, Inter Press Service.

in developing innovative technologies to save and clean water as well. I am particularly excited about innovations that apply biological science to technology—harnessing the power and processes of nature to transform toxic and industrial waste into clean water and even fuel— and the commitment of some businesses of reducing their water use.

However, the private sector must not be allowed to set water policy nor should the market determine who gets access to it. Corporate control of water would see water go to those who can buy it, not to those who need it. It would also encourage the plunder of water from nature, already a terrible problem. It would discourage conservation and source protection, arguably the first step in protecting the world's diminishing water supplies.

Everyone Needs and Deserves Water

What we need now are guiding principles that set priorities for water. Water is a public trust that belongs to the Earth and all species. It is a basic human right. Yes, there is a commercial dimension to water. But the only possible path to a water secure future is based on the twin foundations of conservation and justice. All water use, public and private, must now serve these goals.

EVALUATING THE AUTHOR'S ARGUMENTS:

In the viewpoint you just read, Maude Barlow uses history, facts, and examples to make her argument that access to water is a human right. She does not, however, use any quotations to support her points. If you were to rewrite this article and insert quotations, what authorities might you quote from? Where would you place these quotations to bolster the points Barlow makes?

Access to Clean Water Is Not a Human Right

Alex Robson

"Water is not a 'human right', because supplying it to one person means that someone else has missed out on consuming that water."

Water should not be regarded as a human right, Alex Robson argues in the following viewpoint. He contends that, unlike freedom, water should not be counted among human rights. If one person is granted freedom, Robson says, there is still plenty of freedom to go around for others. But water is finite—when one person drinks water, there is less available for someone else. As such, Robson says water cannot be considered a "public good" but a private one. He says treating water as if it should or can be consumed by everyone will cause it to be overused and wasted. For these reasons, Robson concludes that water should not be regarded as a human right.

Robson is a lecturer in economics at Australian National University.

AS YOU READ, CONSIDER THE FOLLOWING QUESTIONS:

1. According to the author, what is a public good?
2. Why is water often labeled as a public good, according to Robson?
3. What does Robson say happens when one person consumes one liter of water?

Alex Robson, "A 'Public Good' Is Not Just Something Which Is 'Good for the Public,'" *Institute of Public Affairs Review,* July 2007, pp. 39–40. Reproduced by permission.

I n economics, terms such as 'public good', 'monopoly' and 'market failure' have very precise definitions. But a quick glance through one's favourite newspaper reveals that these terms are used carelessly or incorrectly time and again. The result is that policy debates end up mired in confusion, dishonesty and downright stupidity.

Understanding the Concept of Public Goods

Take 'public goods' for example. These are simply goods which simultaneously provide benefits to more than one individual (or, as economists say, they exhibit 'non-rivalry' in consumption). My consumption of a public good does not reduce your ability to enjoy it at the same time; whereas my consumption of a private good automatically eliminates the possibility that you can simultaneously enjoy it. The inability to exclude consumers ('non-excludability') from consuming the good is also sometimes included by economists as part of the definition of 'publicness'.

According to the author, even though people the world over benefit from its use, access to water is not a human right because it is not infinite, like freedom.

Notice that this characterisation of public goods does not refer to how many people purchase the good, the economy's institutional arrangements (socialist dictatorship or free market capitalism?) or the identity of the person supplying the good (private sector or public sector?)

Although economists use it rather sparingly, the term 'public good' is much abused in popular debate, where one finds confusing, contradictory definitions to be the rule rather than the exception. To add to the confusion, the definitions are often not stated explicitly but are usually revealed by the kinds of goods which are classified as being 'public'.

Water is a common example. Often, water seems to be labelled as a public good simply because it is something which members of the public enjoy consuming or consume on a regular basis. Left-wing activists even go so far as to claim that water is a 'basic human right'.

But when a litre of water is consumed by one person, exactly one litre less is available for someone else to consume. And—as anyone who has ever forgotten to pay their water bill would know—it is relatively easy for water suppliers to exclude households from consuming water.

In other words, water is a perfectly rivalrous, perfectly excludable, pure private good and is about as a far from the definition of 'public good' as we can get. The fact that something is consumed by many people and provides each of them with significant benefits does not make it a public good.

Water Is Not a Human Right

Water is not a 'human right', because supplying it to one person means that someone else has missed out on consuming that water. In turn, this means that if I have a 'human right' to consume water, someone else must have an obligation to supply it to me—at their own expense, of course.

Applying this ridiculous definition would lead us to conclude that the entire spectrum of goods, from food and clothing to pencils and

Not Everyone Can Have Equal Access to Water

Fresh water is a finite resource—in fact, only 1 percent of the water on earth is usable. As such, some argue that water is a commodity and not something that can be shared equally by everyone, such as air or freedom.

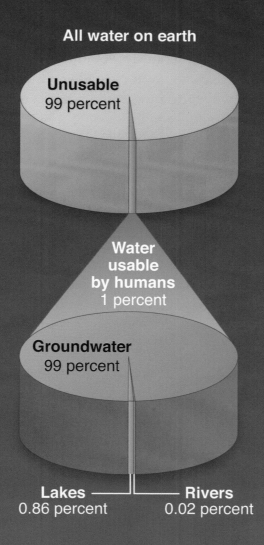

All water on earth

Unusable
99 percent

Water usable by humans
1 percent

Groundwater
99 percent

Lakes ——— **Rivers**
0.86 percent   0.02 percent

Taken from: U.S. Department of the Interior, U.S. Geological Survey, March 4, 2009.
http://ga.water.usps.gov/edu/earthwherewater.html.

paper—basically anything that people consume in sufficiently large amounts or sufficiently regularly—are public goods.

Often, it is the sad reality that governments own and control water resources that seems to drive the view that water is a public good. In other words, according to this approach, a public good is 'something which is owned, produced or provided for by the government'.

This is just as absurd as the first incorrect definition, and the consequences of applying it in practice are rather troubling. Since one of the largest items in the modern government's budget is the basic cash transfer payment (for unemployment benefits, pensions and so on) taking this definition seriously would lead us to conclude that the provision of purchasing power over all goods and services is also a public good—in which case we would again conclude that pretty much everything is a public good.

Governments do indeed own, produce or provide for a vast number of goods and services, but very few of these are actually public goods. . . .

Making Water a Human Right Will Waste It

Politicians, bureaucrats and commentators do indeed attempt to justify government provision of some goods because they fear that individuals will not consume sufficient amounts if left to their own devices. But this is based on a paternalistic view of individuals and on one's definition of 'adequate'. It has little analytical utility and can often lead to contradictions.

For example, a politician might take the view that an individual left to his own devices might consume too little education and too much water. According to the foregoing definition, this would lead us to conclude that education is a public good—but that water is not. And yet it is highly doubtful that the same politician would be willing to leave the allocation of water resources to the forces of the free market.

Why does any of this matter? History tells us that any attempt to 'democratise' water consumption, and transform it from a purely private resource into a 'human right' which must be provided at zero price no matter what, leads to a common pool resource problem in which water is wasted and over-consumed.

In other words, treating private goods as if they were public is a sure recipe for economic disaster. And constantly trying to persuade consumers that they have a right to as much water as they want at zero price by incorrectly using terms such as 'public good' can have grave economic consequences.

EVALUATING THE AUTHORS' ARGUMENTS:

Robson and Barlow (the author of the previous viewpoint) disagree on whether access to water qualifies as a human right. What do you think? Should all humans be guaranteed access to clean, fresh water, or is water a commodity, like food or health care, that people need to pay for? Explain your position using evidence from the viewpoints you have read.

Abortion Is a Human Right

Patty Skuster

"*Abortion is linked to the right to the highest attainable standard of health, the right to privacy, the right to be free of cruel, inhuman or degrading treatment and the right to make decisions about one's reproductive health and life.*"

In the following viewpoint Patty Skuster argues that access to safe, legal abortion is a human right. When women are denied access to abortion, she says, their fundamental right to exercise control over their bodies, along with their right to quality medical care, are sacrificed. When women are denied access to abortion services, they are forced to seek dangerous, life-threatening abortions or give birth to children they are not mentally or financially prepared to raise. It is for this reason, she says, that numerous human rights councils and courts have urged governments to legalize abortion. Skuster concludes that having access to safe, affordable abortion services is a human right for women all over the world.

Skuster is a senior policy advisor at Ipas, an international reproductive rights organization that works to end deaths and injuries from unsafe abortion.

This article appears with permission from Ipas and is adapted from Patty Skuster, "Abortion Is a Human Rights Issue," in *A: The Abortion Magazine*, Winter 2008, pp. 2–3.

AS YOU READ, CONSIDER THE FOLLOWING QUESTIONS:
1. What did the UN General Assembly agree about in 1999, as reported by the author?
2. Who is Karen Llantoy, and how does she factor into the author's argument?
3. According to Skuster, what has the Human Rights Committee recognized as an issue of the right to life?

Human rights ensure that governments do not discriminate based on sex, race, economic status or other characteristics in their efforts to improve or influence people's health and lives. Abortion is linked to the right to the highest attainable standard of health, the right to privacy, the right to be free of cruel, inhuman or degrading treatment and the right to make decisions about one's reproductive health and life, as protected by international agreements. For advocates of access to safe abortion, human rights not only help to hold governments accountable, but also guide and unify advocates from diverse areas and political backgrounds under a common goal.

A Woman's Ultimate Right: Control Over Her Body

The understanding of a woman's human right to decide when and if to have children has evolved and grown over the past 40 years. At the international level, governments recognized the right to make child-bearing decisions at the first global meeting on human rights, as articulated in the 1968 Proclamation of Teheran. The 1979 Convention on the Elimination of all Forms of Discrimination Against Women (CEDAW), was the first international human-rights treaty to explicitly mention family planning. At the 1994 International Conference on Population and Development, 179 governments agreed that free and informed decisionmaking about pregnancy and childbirth is a basic right. In 1999, the U.N. [United Nations] General Assembly agreed that, "where abortion is not against the law, health systems should . . . ensure that such abortion is safe and accessible."

In nearly every country, abortion is legal in some circumstances. But no abortion law by itself can ensure that a woman can safely terminate a pregnancy that is unwanted, damaging to her health or

Americans Believe Women Have the Right to an Abortion

A majority of Americans consistently believe that it is a woman's fundamental right to have access to safe abortion services.

"In general, do you agree or disagree with the 1973 *Roe v. Wade* Supreme Court decision that established a woman's right to an abortion?"

Year of Survey	Percentage Agree	Percentage Disagree	Percentage Unsure
2008	63	33	5
2007	62	32	6
2005	65	30	6

Taken from: Quinnipiac University poll, July 8–13, 2008.

dangerous to her life. The health of these women, and even their lives, can depend on their ability to access safe abortion services. More than 66,000 women die worldwide each year because they are unable to receive safe abortion services, and five million more are hospitalized from complications of unsafe abortion. These women are disproportionately young, poor, women of color, and in positions of low or reduced power.

A Fundamental, International Right

Recognizing abortion as a human-rights issue has recently acquired increasing legal significance. In 2005, the United Nations Human Rights Committee determined that the human rights of Karen Llantoy, a Peruvian woman, were violated when her government denied her a legal termination of her pregnancy. She sought an abortion because of her anencephalic pregnancy [a fatal birth defect that can be detected in the second trimester of pregnancy]. Though doctors confirmed that her baby would die if she carried the pregnancy to term, she was unable to obtain the requisite authorization for an abortion. She gave birth to a girl who survived only four days. Llantoy suffered a severe depression and described her experience as an "extended funeral." The United Nations Human Rights Committee decided that the Peruvian government, in denying Llantoy an abortion, had violated her human rights, including her rights to privacy and to be free of cruel, inhuman or degrading treatment. The decision marked the first time an international body recognized abortion as a human-rights issue in a legal opinion.

Regional human-rights bodies have also recognized abortion as a human-rights issue. The 2003 Protocol on the Rights of Women in Africa to the African Charter on Human and People's Rights requires governments to authorize abortion in certain cases. The European Court of Human Rights recognized that a woman's rights to privacy and freedom from discrimination were violated when the Polish government refused to authorize a legal abortion.

At the national level, in a landmark case decided in 2006, Colombia's Constitutional Court found that the country's restrictive Colombian abortion law violated international human-rights standards.

Safe Abortion Is Critical for Women's Health

The linkages between abortion and human rights have evolved through the work of committees of experts responsible for monitoring the major international human-rights treaties. The Human Rights Committee has recognized the problem of unsafe abortion as an issue of the right to life. The committee that oversees the Convention on the Rights of the Child has urged governments to enact programs to provide safe abortion services where abortion is not against the law. In their recommendation on women and health, the

> **FAST FACT**
>
> The Universal Declaration of Human Rights, the European Commission on Human Rights, conference documents from the United Nations International Conference on Population and Development of 1994 in Cairo, Egypt, and the Fourth World Conference on Women in Beijing, China, in 1995 all express some level of support for viewing access to safe, legal abortion as a human right.

Women's Committee called for decriminalizing abortion, under the Women's Convention. The majority of international human-rights expert committees, in their observations to specific governments, have identified unsafe abortion or lack of access to safe abortion as a human-rights issue.

Safe abortion services are necessary to ensure that women can reach the highest attainable standard of health. Several United Nations Human Rights treaties, including the Universal Declaration of Human Rights, articulate the right to health. The Covenant on Economic, Social and Cultural Rights guarantees the right to the highest attainable standard of physical and mental health, with equity and non-discrimination. In 2004, the United Nations Special Rapporteur on the Right to Health, appointed by the then–United Nations Commission on Human Rights, made explicit the need for abortion services so that governments fulfill the right to health, writing that "where abortions are legal, they must be safe: public-health systems should train and equip health-service providers and take other measures to ensure that such abortions are not only safe but accessible."

Lebanese feminists hold a sit-in on March 8, 2009, in Beirut to support women's right to access abortion services.

High-level recognition of abortion as a human-rights issue strengthens the work of advocates and influences governments to move toward eliminating barriers to abortion services. By acting as human-rights advocates, abortion-rights advocates become part of a larger movement to promote the inherent dignity and equality of all people.

EVALUATING THE AUTHOR'S ARGUMENTS:

Patty Skuster frames abortion as a women's health issue and as a privacy matter, saying women have a right to make medical decisions about their bodies. Do you agree? Why or why not?

Abortion Is a Violation of Human Rights

Derek Remus

"Abortion directly violates the right that is the foundation of all other rights: the right to life."

Derek Remus is a student from Coaldale, Alberta, Canada. His viewpoint was one of three cowinning essays for the 2007 Father Ted Colleton Scholarship Award. In the following viewpoint Remus argues that abortion violates human rights. He considers abortion to be a form of murder—and all forms of murder, he says, are widely viewed as a violation of the ultimate right: the right to life. He views legalized abortion as one of the gravest human rights abuses of our day and warns that true human rights will never be achieved for humanity unless the unborn are guaranteed the right to life.

AS YOU READ, CONSIDER THE FOLLOWING QUESTIONS:

1. According to Remus, what is the right to life rooted in?
2. To what does Remus compare "abortuaries," or abortion clinics?
3. In what way does Remus think failure to believe in God degrades human life?

Derek Remus, "The Most Important Human Rights Violation," *The Interim*, April 2007. Reproduced by permission.

I am 17 years old and have now attended seven election forums in my lifetime—five federal, one provincial and one partisan. At every one of them, candidates and members of the audience have brought up many different matters, a great deal of them trivial. Seldom has anyone brought up that matter which is of such importance that it can clearly be called the most important human rights issue of our day: abortion. And when one does bring it up, one does not have a pleasant reception. At nearly every forum, I have asked the candidates what they will do to stop the killing of unborn children and, once when I asked such a question, an older woman in the audience shouted that I was "sickening."

Abortion Violates the Right to Life

Abortion is an evil to which our culture is now totally desensitized. That is why we must state now more than ever why abortion is the most pressing human rights abuse of our time. In brief, abortion directly violates the right that is the foundation of all other rights: the right to life.

The right to life is the "moral claim that a person has" to exist. It is rooted in the intrinsic dignity of the human person as a creature that God has created in his own image and destined for eternal beatitude. It therefore comes directly from God and can be taken away by no human power; it is a natural, inalienable right.

The human person indeed possesses other natural rights (such as liberty and private property), but the right to life is prior to them all,

> **FAST FACT**
>
> Since abortion ends a pregnancy, antiabortionists view the roughly 49 million abortions that have taken place in the United States since *Roe v. Wade* legalized abortion in 1973 as 49 million acts of murder.

because without it, these other rights could not possibly be exercised. Liberty and property are not much good if one is dead.

Furthermore, the right to life is prior to all positive rights (those goods that are given by a government to its citizens), since natural rights as a whole are prior to positive rights, inasmuch as natural rights come from God and positive rights come only from the state.

Religious protestors who oppose abortion argue that the right to life is the ultimate human right.

Therefore, the right to life is the most fundamental of all rights. Consequently, the violation of the right to life is the most fundamental of all violations of rights. And abortion is precisely that: the violation of the right to life—the cold-blooded killing of an innocent human person.

Abortion Is Murder

It is an indisputable fact, rooted in science, philosophy and divine revelation, that personhood begins at conception and that the union of the sperm and the egg is a new being composed of a body and a rational soul, "the seed of eternity we bear within ourselves." Personhood is independent of and prior to any functions that one performs. "He who will one day be a man is a man already."

Thus, abortion is an offence no different than the murder of a born person. Over time, I have realized more and more that we are living in a time not unlike that of Nazi Germany or Soviet Russia. I have realized that the Morgentaler Kensington abortuary [an abortion clinic] in Calgary (near where I live) is no less evil than [Adolf] Hitler and [Joseph] Stalin's concentration camps. But the massacres committed by Nazism and Soviet communism were confined to areas under German and Russian control. Abortion, the massacre committed by relativism, is a global evil.

Indeed, the number of abortions that occur in the world is massive. According to the Guttmacher Institute, the research arm of Planned Parenthood, 46 million abortions were committed worldwide in 1995. But in addition to this number is the countless number of children killed through abortifacient contraceptives. "Throughout the world, an estimated 250 million abortions are caused by the IUD [intrauterine device] and pill each year." In the words of Monsignor Vincent N. Foy, Canadian priest and canon lawyer, "Is it an exaggeration to describe the world as a slaughterhouse?"

Denying the Divinity in Life

Last year, I read *Memory and Identity*, the last book by Pope John Paul II. In this book, the Holy Father stated that at the root of the widespread slaughter of abortion is the rejection of God as self-existent being and supreme Creator, as the One who alone can tell us what is right and wrong. After recently reading Father John A. Hardon's *Atheistic Communism: The Destruction of Human Person, Family, Civilized*

"Life-ectomy," cartoon by Gary McCoy, April 24, 2007. Copyright © 2007 by Gary McCoy and PoliticalCartoons.com. All rights reserved.

Society, I realize that in this rejection of God we can clearly see the quintessential role of Marxist communism in creating the culture of death. Communism denies the existence of God and the immortality of the soul and thus, holds that the human person is a mere blob of matter who has no intrinsic dignity or "divine rights to be born alive." All that the individual person has are the benefits given him (and therefore capable of being taken away from him) by the "collectivity."

Is this usurpation of God by the state not precisely what we see when governments arbitrate to themselves the authority to determine that certain human beings shall have the right to live and others (such as the unborn) shall not?

Therefore, when we speak of abortion as the greatest human rights issue of our day, we are speaking of something far more grave than a "merely constitutional issue of civil rights." We are speaking of man undermining the most fundamental of all the rights God has invested in the human person.

Furthermore, when abortion is accepted (and, by necessity, contraception and sterilization, abortion's bedfellows, as well), numerous other attacks against human rights, both the right to life and other rights, will inevitably follow. . . .

I will conclude with the words of Pope John Paul II: "If the right to life is not defended decisively as a condition for all other rights of the person, all other references to human rights remain deceitful and illusory." Abortion, the direct violation of the inalienable right to life, is the most important human rights violation of our day, against which we must fight until it is totally abolished.

EVALUATING THE AUTHOR'S ARGUMENTS:

Remus uses religion to frame his argument that abortion violates human rights. Summarize the role religion plays in his argument. Then, state whether you agree with him on whether abortion violates human rights.

Chapter 2

Are Human Rights Protected Worldwide?

Human rights activists protest in Tokyo, Japan, May 30, 2009, over human rights abuses by the Myanmar government and the detention of pro-democracy activist Aung San Suu Kyi.

The United States Is a Beacon of Human Rights

> "Americans, in general, think—and act—on human rights because liberty is their foundational value and they have an instinctive hatred of oppression."

America in the World

In the following viewpoint analysts from the London Centre for the Study of Anti-Americanism argue that the United States is the greatest champion of human rights in the world. They claim that the United States has done more than any other nation— from foreign policy to international aid and programs to official documents—to protect and promote human rights both at home and abroad. They think those who criticize the United States for abusing human rights need to realize that no country is perfect and no country has done more consistent human rights promotion than the United States.

The London Centre for the Study of Anti-Americanism is an organization that seeks to increase understanding of America, debunk myths about the United States, and make the case for why America should retain a continuing leading role in the world.

America in the World, "America and Human Rights," America in the World's Briefings, August 2008. Reproduced by permission.

In the wake of Abu Ghraib [an Iraqi prison where American soldiers tortured Iraqi inmates], Guantanamo Bay [a detention center in Cuba where detainees in the war on terror are held, some for years at a time] and the [George W.] Bush Administration's lack of clarity on practices such as 'water-boarding', considered by many to be torture, the United States has been widely criticised on human rights issues. The US has become regarded by many as somewhat hypocritical—and for the most strident anti-Americans, the US is talked of as a human rights abuser far more frequently than North Korea, Burma or Sudan.

No Country Has Done More for Human Rights

Such criticisms, however, represent an extraordinary loss of perspective. While incidents such as Abu Ghraib are abhorrent, and rendition and torture in the war on terror raise serious questions, no country has done more, overall, to promote democracy and human rights around the world than the United States. Alongside abuses that both 2008 presidential candidates are pledged to end, America's role in overthrowing evil regimes in Afghanistan and Iraq—and safeguarding Kosovo—have to be placed in the credit column.

Moreover, unlike most non-democratic regimes, the human rights abuses are exceptional rather than systematic, and in fact the United States has within its very system the means of ending abuses that do occur. The United States can be criticised for inconsistency, given its past support for some dictatorships, and condemned for hypocrisy, but dissidents and human rights activists will struggle to find a more helpful, pro-active champion than America. In its rhetoric, policies, programmes, legislation and government structures, democracy and human rights promotion is a central feature of US foreign policy. Even if it does not always live up to its ideals, it is streets ahead of most European countries in this field. The record of the Czechs, Dutch and Scandinavians are good, but they lack the clout of the USA.

From its founding fathers through to the current [Bush] Administration, the US has spoken of liberty far more clearly and frequently than most other nations. Thomas Jefferson wrote in the Declaration of Independence those crucial words describing all men as equal and endowed with "inalienable" rights long before the Universal Declaration of Human Rights was conceived. The Constitution's first amendment, introduced by James Madison and effective from 1791, states: "Congress shall make no law respecting an establishment of religion, or prohibiting the free exercise thereof; or abridging the freedom of speech, or of the press; or the right of the people peaceably to assemble, and to petition the Government for a redress of grievances."

FAST FACT

France, Germany, Britain, Poland, Russia, Turkey, Egypt, Lebanon, Jordan, South Korea, India, Indonesia, China, Pakistan, Argentina, Brazil, and Tanzania are all among countries that the Pew Global Attitudes Project found in 2008 held more favorable opinions of the United States than in the previous year.

Virtually every US President has made speeches promoting freedom, far more boldly than European leaders. It is in their "DNA". Some have made human rights a more particular focus than others, notably Presidents Jimmy Carter and Ronald Reagan. In 1982 President Reagan told the British Parliament: "We must be staunch in our conviction that freedom is not the sole prerogative of a lucky few but the inalienable and universal right of all human beings." He continued by paying tribute to Britain for its contribution to advancing "individual liberty, representative government and the rule of law" but then added a challenge. He said: "I have often wondered about the shyness of some of us in the West about standing for these ideals that have done so much to ease the plight of man and the hardships of our imperfect world. . . . Let us ask ourselves: what kind of people do we think we are? And let us answer: free people, worthy of freedom, and determined not only to remain so but to help others gain their freedom as well. . . . Let us now begin a major effort to secure the best—a crusade for freedom that will engage the faith and fortitude of the next generation. For the sake of peace and justice, let us move toward a world in which all people are at last free to determine their own destiny."

And the [former] Secretary of State Condoleezza Rice, although schooled in the "realist" approach to foreign policy, said in 2005: "We have a great opportunity to spread freedom and democracy as an antidote to this ideology of terror". . . .

The U.S. Government Is Hardwired for Rights Protection

Human rights issues are hardwired into US Government structures. Within the US State Department, there is an Under Secretary of State for Democracy and Global Affairs, who has responsibility for human rights—overseeing the work of the Bureau of Democracy, Labour and Human Rights, headed by an Assistant Secretary of State. These structures were established by President Jimmy Carter. Critics argue that "DRL" as it is known is buried within the State Department apparatus, and does not have enough input into decisions made by the main power-brokers, the country desks and regional bureaus. Critics argue that human rights promotion has not yet been fully integrated into the mainstream of the State Department. That may be so, but even in having such a bureau the US is rare compared with other governments. The State Department produces annual reports on human rights, religious freedom and trafficking in persons, a report on advancing freedom and democracy, and has various special offices and representatives, such as the Office of International Religious Freedom, headed by an Ambassador-at-Large, the Office to Monitor and Combat Trafficking in Persons, also led by an Ambassador-at-Large, and similar mandates for war crimes and women's issues. Once again, critics claim these do not wield the influence they should—but compared with other governments, the fact that such sections even exist, and are as well-staffed as they are, puts the US way ahead of others.

Congress also has powers to promote human rights and freedom. The US is unusual in having legislative power over foreign policy. In most parliamentary systems, the legislature can raise questions, write letters and seek to influence foreign policy, but in the US Congress has the power to pass foreign policy laws with which the State Department may disagree. The International Religious Freedom Act, for example, was passed unanimously by Congress in 1998, creating the Office of International Religious Freedom in the State Department, and a watch-dog body, the US Commission on International Religious Freedom, to monitor the State Department's performance in promoting religious liberty around the world. Numerous bills on specific countries, such as Sudan, North Korea and Burma, are passed by Congress, imposing sanctions and mandating the Administration to take particular actions to promote human rights. Congress has a good number of members who consistently champion human rights, and travel to places of oppression and persecution—men such as Senators Sam Brownback or John McCain or Congressmen Frank Wolf, Christopher Smith, Joseph Pitts and the recently deceased Tom Lantos.

In addition to the administration and legislature, the US has many government-funded democracy-promotion programmes. The National Endowment for Democracy (NED) is perhaps the most significant, but the two major political parties have their own international democracy-promotion arms—the International Republican Institute (currently chaired by senator John McCain) and the National Democratic Institute.

The World's Best Human Rights Groups Come from the United States

Outside government, the US has given birth to some of the world's best human rights non-governmental organizations. Human Rights Watch, Freedom House, Human Rights First and International Justice Mission are just four names to mention. Washington, DC and New York house numerous human rights organisations, ranging from specialist campaigns on country-specific issues, such as North Korea, China, Tibet, Burma or Sudan, to thematic organisations focused on themes such as religious freedom, human trafficking

In addition to government agencies, the United States has many private human rights organizations such as the Carter Institute, started by former president Jimmy Carter.

or freedom of expression. The Carter Institute, founded by former President Jimmy Carter, does valuable work promoting democracy and human rights, and monitoring elections. And unlike British think tanks, most of which focus on a specific area of policy—either economic or social—almost all the major American think-tanks include a significant focus on foreign policy, and within that the promotion of liberty. Their leanings may vary, but the Heritage Foundation, the American Enterprise Institute, the Hudson Institute and the Brookings [Institution] all publish pamphlets and lectures on human rights in foreign policy.

On a less tangible, more personal level, Americans—in and out of government—tend, generally, to show more interest, and more desire to help, in international human rights issues than any other nation. Of course that is a generalisation, and there are plenty of exceptions: disinterested and unhelpful Americans, and helpful, committed Europeans. Nevertheless, on average the responsiveness—and pro-activeness—of American officials in the State Department, staffers and elected representatives in Congress, think-tank policy advisers, media and members of the public, is far greater than in any other country. Americans, in general, think—and act—on human rights because liberty is their foundational value and they have an instinctive hatred of oppression.

EVALUATING THE AUTHORS' ARGUMENTS:

The London Centre for the Study of Anti-Americanism argues that if the United States has abused human rights, these mistakes have been rare and random. How do you think Human Rights Watch, the author of the following viewpoint, would respond to this claim?

The United States Violates Human Rights

Human Rights Watch

"Resistance to scrutiny of . . . counterterrorism policies and past abuses continues to be a major obstacle to human rights improvement in the United States."

In the following viewpoint, excerpted from a longer article, Human Rights Watch argues that the United States routinely violates the human rights of both Americans and noncitizens. The author explains how the administration of former president George W. Bush introduced policies that allowed officials to use torture to deal with enemies or suspected terrorists. But according to Human Rights Watch, it is never acceptable to torture suspected or convicted criminals. The organization also argues that criminals in the United States are subjected to cruel and unusual punishment when they are denied adequate medical care or their right to privacy and safety and when they are executed for their crimes. Women, especially, according to Human Rights Watch, do not fully enjoy human rights in the United States.

Human Rights Watch is one of the world's leading independent organizations dedicated to defending and protecting human rights.

AS YOU READ, CONSIDER THE FOLLOWING QUESTIONS:
1. According to the author, what techniques did the Department of Justice authorize in 2005?
2. What percentage of prisoner deaths in California does Human Rights Watch say were preventable?
3. In what ways did women's rights suffer setbacks in 2007, according to the author?

Events of 2007

Bush administration resistance to scrutiny of its counterterrorism policies and past abuses continues to be a major obstacle to human rights improvement in the United States. Despite some efforts in Congress to change practices violating basic human rights, there was no evident progress concerning the treatment of so-called enemy combatants, including those held at Guantánamo Bay, or the use of secret detention facilities.

Domestically, undocumented migrant workers faced an increased risk of detention, and other non-citizens were blocked from vindicating their rights in court. Persons convicted of crimes faced harsh sentencing policies and in some cases abusive conditions in US prisons.

Racial discrimination again emerged as a prominent issue in 2007, when six African-American high school students in Jena, Louisiana, were charged as adults with a range of serious crimes for the 2006 beating of a white student. The case sparked protests and the charges were widely viewed as excessive and discriminatory, especially as compared with the treatment of white Jena youths involved in other incidents. . . .

Torture Policy

Over the past two years, Congress and the courts have repudiated the Bush administration's authorization of abusive interrogation techniques that amount to torture. In response the Pentagon announced new rules applicable to all interrogations carded out by the United States armed forces and disavowed many abusive techniques. The Central Intelligence Agency (CIA), however, contends that it is not bound by these rules, and the administration has gone to great lengths to justify the CIA's continued use of certain techniques banned for use by the military. According to an October 2007 *New York Times* article, the Department of Justice issued legal memoranda in 2005 that authorized the use of waterboarding (simulated drowning), head slapping, and exposure to frigid temperatures, and ruled that neither

Anti-torture activists say the use of waterboarding to extract information from prisoners is a violation of human rights. The practice has been used by the United States at the Guantánamo Bay detention facility in Cuba.

these techniques, nor any other techniques being employed by the CIA, violated the then-pending legislation prohibiting cruel, inhuman, and degrading treatment. In October 2007 the Bush administration's candidate for attorney general, Michael Mukasey, refused to repudiate waterboarding as a form of torture in his confirmation hearings.

In July 2007 the administration issued an executive order providing legal authorization for the so-called "CIA program" in which detainees are held incommunicado and subject to reportedly abusive interrogations. Michael McConnell, Director of National Intelligence, said on July 22, 2007 that he "would not want a US citizen to go through the process" of being subjected to some of the techniques approved for use by the CIA.

FAST FACT

According to a 2009 CNN poll, 60 percent of Americans would characterize the George W. Bush administration's use of harsh interrogation tactics, such as waterboarding, as torture.

Secret Prisons

In April 2007 the Department of Defense announced the transfer to Guantanamo of another detainee who was previously held in CIA custody, suggesting that secret prisons (temporarily closed after President Bush's admission that they existed in 2006) were up and running again. Human Rights Watch has identified 39 other people we believe were held in secret prisons; administration officials have indicated the total number to be about 100. Under international law those persons remain unlawfully "disappeared" until the United States can account for them. In July President Bush issued an executive order providing authorization for this "CIA program," despite the patent illegality of incommunicado detention under international law. . . .

Incarceration

There are more than 2.2 million persons in US prisons and jails, an increase of 500 percent from 30 years ago. A June 2007 report by the Justice Department's Bureau of Justice Statistics (BJS) found that the incarcerated population continued to grow in 2006, experiencing its largest one-year increase in six years. The United States now has both the largest incarcerated population and the highest per capita incarceration rate in the world, with a rate five times that of England and Wales, seven times that of Canada, and more than 10 times that of Japan.

The burden of incarceration falls disproportionately on members of racial and ethnic minorities. Black men are incarcerated at 6.5 times the rate of white men, and 11.7 percent of all black males age 25 to 29 are in prison or jail. The US government failed to explain or address these rates in its 2007 report to the United Nations Committee on the Elimination of Racial Discrimination, hearings on which are expected in February 2008.

As the prison population grows, so does the challenge of providing adequate medical and mental health care. A September 2006 BJS report found that more than half of all prisoners—and nearly three-quarters of all female prisoners—suffer from a mental health problem such as major depression or a psychotic disorder.

In California a federal judge found that medical care in the state's prisons violated the US Constitution's prohibition on cruel and unusual punishment. In 2006 the judge appointed a receiver to oversee prison medical care, stripping that function from the state government. In September 2007 the receiver issued a report finding that 15 percent of California prisoner deaths were either preventable or possibly preventable.

Enacted by the US Congress in 1996, the Prison Litigation Reform Act (PLRA) creates a variety of obstacles for prisoners seeking to challenge their conditions of confinement or otherwise vindicate their rights in court. In January 2007 the US Supreme Court issued a decision overturning some particularly restrictive interpretations of the PLRA by lower federal courts.

The Death Penalty and Juvenile Life Without Parole

State governments executed 42 prisoners between January and October 2007, bringing the total number of men and women executed in the

United States to 1099 since 1977. Almost all were killed by lethal injection; one was electrocuted.

With growing evidence that lethal injection may be a very painful way to die, executions in many states were halted in 2007. In September 2007 the US Supreme Court agreed to consider the constitutionality of lethal injection in the case of two Kentucky death row prisoners claiming that lethal injection amounts to cruel and unusual punishment. Lethal injections in the US are expected to decrease substantially until the court issues its decision sometime in 2008.

In 2007 Human Rights Watch revised upward, from 2,225 to at least 2,380, our estimate of the number of US prisoners serving sentences of life without parole for crimes committed when they were under 18. The number of such prisoners in the rest of world combined is eight. Efforts at reforming this excessively punitive sentence for young offenders continued in several states across the country, including in Michigan and California.

Women's Rights

Women's rights in the United States suffered major setbacks at the Supreme Court in 2007. One court decision severely restricted challenges to unequal pay (women earn only 77 cents for every dollar earned by men), another upheld the exclusion of in-home care workers from certain federal wage and overtime protections (89 percent of such workers are women), and a third upheld a ban on a medically approved late-term abortion method, adding to existing regulatory and financial obstacles to safe abortion.

The US continues to channel its international assistance toward programs that compromise sexual and reproductive health and rights. In 2007, a significant portion of US funding for HIV/AIDS prevention continued to be earmarked for programs that promote abstinence until marriage, regardless of whether such programs were likely to be effective and without sufficient regard for abuses that put women, even those who abstain until marriage, at high risk for HIV.

In a positive step, the Senate in 2007 approved a bill that would overturn the "global gag rule"—a series of restrictions on what recipients of US reproductive health aid can do and say on abortion. At this writing, it remained unclear whether the bill would become law. . . .

"Almost Done," cartoon by Tab, *The Calgary Sun,* January 14, 2009, PoliticalCartoons.com. Copyright © 2009 by Tab and PoliticalCartoons.com. All rights reserved.

Sex Offenders

In a 2007 report, *No Easy Answers*, Human Rights Watch found that, as currently conceived, many sex offender registry laws do little to prevent sexual violence and violate fundamental human rights. Offenders on publicly available registries find it difficult to obtain or keep employment and housing. Some have been murdered and many are harassed by strangers who find their information online. Residency restrictions lead to homelessness and transience for some convicted sex offenders, which interfere with their effective tracking, monitoring, and supervision by law enforcement officers; this in turn may make repeat offenses more likely.

Sex offender laws ignore the full reality of sexual violence in the US. Child safety advocates question the focus in current law on "stranger danger" and already convicted offenders because more than 90 percent of child sexual abuse is committed by someone the child knows and trusts. Authoritative studies show that three out of four sex offenders do not re-offend within 15 years of release from prison and 87 percent of sex crimes are committed by individuals without a previous conviction for a sex offense. . . .

EVALUATING THE AUTHOR'S ARGUMENTS:

In this viewpoint Human Rights Watch focuses on how the United States violates the rights of prisoners and ex-convicts. In your opinion, how important is it for society to respect the rights of prisoners? Should people who have violated the law forfeit their human rights, or is extending human rights to all people—no matter what they have done—an important aspect of society? Explain your reasoning.

China Has Improved Its Human Rights Record

Peter Ford

> *"Nothing we do today was possible 25 years ago. Compared with then, the human rights situation in China has improved like never before."*

In the following viewpoint Peter Ford discusses the state of human rights in China prior to the 2008 Olympics in Beijing. He points out several freedoms the Chinese people have today that they did not enjoy twenty-five years ago. For example, the government used to exercise tight control over certain aspects of everyday life, such as one's occupation, travel abroad, private property, business ownership, and entertainment. But today the government allows individuals the freedom to make choices in these areas and to express their personal opinions among family and friends. Ford acknowledges that China is a long way from being as free as the United States, and its citizens are still subject to serious human rights violations. But, Ford suggests that the degree of and commitment to improvement in human rights over the last twenty-five years give reason to hope that China will become even freer and more open as time goes on.

Peter Ford is a staff writer for the *Christian Science Monitor.*

Peter Ford, "Amid Human Rights Protests, a Look at China's Record: Freedoms Have Improved Tremendously in the Past 25 Years, but Chinese People Today Face Plenty of Red Lines," *Christian Science Monitor,* April 10, 2008. Reproduced by permission from *Christian Science Monitor* (www.csmonitor.com).

AS YOU READ, CONSIDER THE FOLLOWING QUESTIONS:
  1. Who is Li Datong, and how does he factor into the author's argument?
  2. According to Ford, how did a person come to work in his or her profession twenty-five years ago in China?
  3. What did a 2006 United Nations report find in regard to Chinese prisons?

The international torch relay for the [2008] Beijing Olympic Games has been besieged in almost every city it has visited so far by protesters against repression in Tibet and human rights violations in China. But what is the human rights picture really like in China, and how has it changed over the past quarter of a century?

As with so much else in China, the situation is mixed, sometimes confused, and often hard to make out with precision. Some observers like to point to the progress China has made toward international norms; others prefer to stress how far it still is from reaching them.

The imminence of the Games, and the Chinese government's effort to use them as a showcase for its achievements, have polarized the debate. Here, the [Christian Science] Monitor tries to cut through the rhetoric with an outline explanation of the key issues.

What Kind of Freedoms Do Chinese People Enjoy in Their Personal Lives?

"Nothing we do today was possible 25 years ago. Compared with then, the human rights situation in China has improved like never before."

And that enthusiastic assessment comes from a man who was fired from his job in 2006 as editor of a Communist youth newspaper for publishing an article that contradicted the party line, Li Datong.

But the baseline, he points out, was pretty low. "In 1983, I would probably have been arrested."

Twenty-five years ago, Chinese citizens were not free to choose their jobs: The authorities assigned them work for life. Farmers were forbidden to live anywhere but the village where they were born. Nobody was allowed to travel abroad, except on government-authorized business. Nobody could dream of owning a car, let alone a house. Food was rationed. Nobody was allowed to set up a business. Western movies and books were banned.

Today, all that has changed. And as the state has relaxed its control over the minutiae of daily life, citizens have also felt freer to express themselves to each other. Among friends and neighbors, Chinese say

At the 2007 Congress of the Communist Party (pictured), China proclaimed that human rights issues are improving in their country.

what they think about everything, from their political leaders to rising prices to their country's medal chances at the Beijing Olympics.

So Where Is the Problem?

The boulevard of freedoms that Chinese people enjoy may have widened, but it is still lined with precipices. You may be able to criticize the ruling Communist Party over dinner with friends, but airing such views in public—for example on the Internet—can earn you years of prison time.

You would not get a chance to run that risk anywhere else: All newspapers and TV and radio stations are owned by the government and edited by men and women who know where the red lines are drawn. Each time a new issue comes up, the Communist Party propaganda department sends them a directive telling them the line to take.

Freedom of speech is guaranteed in the constitution. But it is upheld only for those who do not challenge Communist Party rule. Communist Party security agents decide what constitutes a challenge.

Certainly you cannot call for free elections or a multiparty state, or criticize party leaders by name. Nor can you advocate independence for Tibet, or Taiwan's right to self-rule. Nor can you try to set up an independent trade union.

On other issues, "it's like crossing the stream by feeling where the rocks are," says John Kamm, a human rights advocate who heads the San Francisco–based Dui Hua Foundation.

Citizens who have slipped off the rocks, and ended up in jail, include land rights activists, practitioners of the banned Falun Gong spiritual movement, tenants protesting eviction from their homes by developers, defense lawyers, and Tibetan Buddhists and Muslim Uighurs demanding more respect for their cultures and religions, members of Christian churches not authorized by the state, and anticorruption campaigners, among others.

FAST FACT

A 2008 poll published by the Pew Internet & American Life Project found that more than 80 percent of Chinese citizens think the Internet should be managed or controlled by the government in some way.

Americans Want China to Improve Its Human Rights Record

A survey of Americans showed that most thought it was very important for China to improve its human rights record during the upcoming year.

Over the next year, how important would you say each of the following actions are for China to take?

Action	Very Important %	Fairly Important %	Somewhat Important %	Not That Important %	Unsure %
Improve human rights	73	10	10	4	3
Enact policies that are more protective of the environment	57	14	17	8	4
Open its trading policies to become more fair	55	15	17	9	4

Taken from: NBC News/*Wall Street Journal* poll, July 27–30, 2007.

Often they are convicted of endangering state security by inciting subversion or separatism: Mr. Kamm estimates that 4,000 prisoners are serving sentences for such crimes, of which outsiders know the names of only a few hundred.

Has China's Role as Olympic Host in 2008 Encouraged the Authorities to Improve Their Human Rights Record?

No. If anything it seems to have made things worse, as the Chinese government tries to ensure a "harmonious" event.

The international human rights watchdog Amnesty International says in a recent report that "the crackdown on peaceful activists has intensified as a direct result of China's hosting of the Olympic Games. Several of the activists . . . have been targeted because they have explicitly linked human rights and the Olympics, and have been among the most harshly treated."

The government's own statistics show that 742 people were arrested for "endangering state security" last year—more than double the 2005 figure, and the highest number since 1999.

What Chance of a Fair Trial Do You Stand in China?

Companies with commercial cases before the courts say Chinese judges are becoming more professional and fairer—unless a state-owned business is involved, in which case it can generally expect favorable treatment.

In criminal and political cases, however, sentences are decided not by judges but by a court committee named by the Communist Party. Verdicts sometimes appear to have been reached before the formality of a court hearing: Human rights activist Hu Jia's recent trial lasted only four hours, and his defense lawyer was allowed to speak for just 30 minutes.

At least he had a lawyer, which would have been unthinkable for a dissident 25 years ago. But lawyers taking such cases have to be brave: Advocate Gao Zhisheng was beaten up and abducted for a month last year—apparently by plainclothesmen—after writing an open letter to the US Congress denouncing "China's ongoing human rights disaster." Two other prominent rights lawyers, Teng Biao and Li Heping, have suffered similar fates in recent months: Others have been jailed or put under house arrest.

The Chinese police are not always very particular about how they extract confessions: A United Nations report in 2006 found that torture in police stations was declining but still "widespread."

The police do not always bother to go to court with their suspects. The law allows them to sentence anyone to up to three years of "reeducation through labor," an administrative punishment against which there is no appeal. Local authorities often use it against land rights activists, petitioners drawing Beijing's attention to injustices, and other troublesome types.

How Many People Do Chinese Courts Condemn to Death Each Year?

Nobody knows for sure because the government keeps the figure a secret, but foreign experts with good contacts in the Chinese judiciary estimate that between 5,000 and 6,000 people were given the death penalty last year [2007]. Though 25 countries today practiced capital punishment in 2006, China was by far the heaviest user—it was responsible for two-thirds of the world's confirmed executions, according to Amnesty International.

The Chinese Supreme Court is making an effort to bring the numbers down, by insisting on reviewing all death penalty sentences imposed by lower courts. Ten years ago, as many as 15,000 people a year were being sentenced to death, according to foreign estimates.

Some Chinese academics and jurists have argued publicly in favor of abolishing the death penalty. The authorities have shown no sign of being ready to do that.

EVALUATING THE AUTHORS' ARGUMENTS:

In this viewpoint Ford mentions several positive things about life today in China as well as many negative things. Compare this view with the next viewpoint by the U.S. Department of State, which argues that regard for human rights in China is getting worse. Does the latter viewpoint refer to any of the good things mentioned by Ford? In your opinion, which viewpoint presents the more accurate picture of life in China? Support your answer with evidence from each viewpoint.

China Violates Human Rights

U.S. Department of State

"The [Chinese] government's human rights record remained poor and worsened in some areas."

The following viewpoint was written by the U.S. Department of State. In its *2008 Human Rights Report: China,* the State Department argues that China is a severe violator of human rights. It reports that Chinese citizens are killed and arrested for no compelling reason, their privacy is routinely violated, their news and information are tightly controlled, and they are not free to worship. The State Department chronicles multiple instances in which Chinese citizens have had their human rights violated and says the humanitarian situation in that country is worsening.

AS YOU READ, CONSIDER THE FOLLOWING QUESTIONS:

1. In what ways did Chinese officials reportedly abuse prisoners, according to the State Department?
2. What kinds of people does the State Department say are routinely arrested in China?
3. Name four ways in which the State Department says the Chinese government violates the privacy of its citizens.

U.S. Department of State, "2008 Human Rights Report: China (includes Tibet, Hong Kong, and Macau)," in *Bureau of Democracy, Human Rights, and Labor,* February 25, 2009. Public Domain.

The People's Republic of China, with a population of approximately 1.3 billion, is an authoritarian state in which the Chinese Communist Party (CCP) constitutionally is the paramount source of power. Party members hold almost all top government, police, and military positions. Ultimate authority rests with the 25-member political bureau (Politburo) of the CCP and its nine-member standing committee. Hu Jintao holds the three most powerful positions as CCP general secretary, president, and chairman of the Central Military Commission. Civilian authorities generally maintained effective control of the security forces.

Human Rights Are Worsening in China

[In 2008] the government's human rights record remained poor and worsened in some areas. During the year the government increased its severe cultural and religious repression of ethnic minorities in Tibetan areas and the Xinjiang Uighur Autonomous Region (XUAR), increased detention and harassment of dissidents and petitioners, and maintained tight controls on freedom of speech and the Internet. Abuses peaked around high-profile events, such as the Olympics and the unrest in Tibet. As in previous years, citizens did not have the right to change their government. Nongovernmental organizations (NGOs), both local and international, continued to face intense scrutiny and restrictions. Other serious human rights abuses included extrajudicial killings, torture and coerced confessions of prisoners, and the use of forced labor, including prison labor. Workers cannot choose an independent union to represent them in the workplace, and the law does not protect workers' right to strike.

The government continued to monitor, harass, detain, arrest, and imprison journalists, writers, activists, and defense lawyers and their families, many of whom were seeking to exercise their rights under the law. A lack of due process and restrictions on lawyers further limited progress toward rule of law, with serious consequences for defendants who were imprisoned or executed following proceedings that fell far short of international standards. The party and state exercised strict political control of courts and judges, conducted closed trials, and carried out administrative detention. Individuals and groups, especially those deemed politically sensitive by the government, continued to face tight restrictions on their freedom to assemble, their freedom to practice religion, and their freedom to travel. The government continued its coercive birth limitation policy, in some cases resulting in forced abortion or forced sterilization. The government failed to protect refugees adequately, and the detention and forced repatriation of North Koreans continued to be a problem. Serious social conditions that affected human rights included endemic corruption, trafficking in persons, and discrimination against women, minorities, and persons with disabilities. . . .

Arbitrary, Unlawful Killings

During the year security forces reportedly committed arbitrary or unlawful killings. No official statistics on deaths in custody were available. The outbreak of widespread unrest in the Tibet Autonomous Region (TAR) and other Tibetan areas in March and April [2008] resulted in significant loss of life, with many credible reports putting the number killed at over 200.

On January 7 [2008], Wei Wenhua was beaten to death by municipal "urban management" officials in Tianmen, Hubei Province, after he filmed their clash with local residents on his mobile phone. Authorities detained 41 officials and sentenced four to short prison terms for their role in Wei's death. On February 6, authorities reportedly instructed the family of Falun Gong practitioner Yu Zhou, who had been arrested in Beijing on January 26, to come to an emergency center to see him. Yu was dead when the family arrived, and authorities claimed he had died of diabetes. However, Yu's family stated that he was healthy at the time of his arrest and that authorities refused the family's request for an autopsy. On May 26, the family of Tibetan protester Paltsal Kyab was informed he died in custody, after he was detained in April for participating in a March 17 protest. Authorities claimed Paltsal Kyab had died from kidney and stomach problems, although relatives reported he was healthy at the time of his arrest. According to witnesses his body was covered with bruises and burn blisters. There were no reports of any official investigation into his death. On July 16, 100 individuals reportedly attacked police

Chinese police officers deploy near Tiananmen Square on June 4, 2009, determined to halt a demonstration commemorating the twentieth anniversary of the massacre that occurred there in 1989.

in Huizhou, Guangdong Province, after a motorcyclist died. Police reported the man died in a traffic accident but his relatives claimed he was beaten to death by security guards. . . .

Torture and Unacceptable Conditions for Detainees and Prisoners

The law prohibits the physical abuse of detainees and forbids prison guards from extracting confessions by torture, insulting prisoners' dignity, and beating or encouraging others to beat prisoners. However, during the year there were reports that officials used electric shocks, beatings, shackles, and other forms of abuse.

Mao Hengfeng, a family planning issues petitioner, reportedly was physically and mentally abused in prison. During an August 13 [2008] phone call, Mao reportedly told her husband that scars on her wrists that resulted from being tied up tightly had not healed.

On May 22, Heilongjiang resident and reform activist Liu Jie was transferred from a Qiqihar reeducation through labor (RTL) camp to the Harbin Drug Rehabilitation Center, where she reportedly was tortured. Human rights organizations also reported democracy activist and member of the China Democracy Party (CDP) Chi Jianwei reportedly was tortured in July 2007 for refusing to confess to "using an evil cult to hinder law enforcement."

In November [2008] the UN [United Nations] Committee Against Torture (UNCAT) stated its deep concern about the routine and widespread use of torture and ill-treatment of suspects in police custody, especially to extract confessions or information used in criminal proceedings. However, UNCAT did acknowledge government efforts to address the practice of torture and related problems in the criminal justice system. Many alleged acts of torture occurred in pretrial criminal detention centers or RTL centers. Sexual and physical abuse and extortion occurred in some detention centers. . . .

Conditions in penal institutions for both political prisoners and common criminals generally were harsh and often degrading. Prisoners and detainees often were kept in overcrowded conditions with poor sanitation. Inadequate prison capacity was an increasing problem in some areas. Food often was inadequate and of poor quality, and many detainees relied on supplemental food and medicines provided by relatives; some prominent dissidents were not allowed to receive such goods.

FAST FACT

Because China does not tolerate privacy, oppresses political opposition, censors criticism of the state, and punishes people for thinking and acting independently, it was ranked in 2009 as "Not Free" by the human rights organization Freedom House.

Many inmates in penal and RTL facilities were required to work, with minimal or no remuneration. In some cases prisoners worked in facilities directly connected with penal institutions; in other cases they were contracted to nonprison enterprises. Former prison inmates reported that workers who refused to work in some prisons were beaten. Facilities and their management profited from inmate labor.

Chinese Citizens Are Not Free

China severely violates its people's rights, according to several major human rights watch groups.

Death penalty

China executes more people each year than the rest of the world put together. A Chinese legal scholar estimates about 8,000 are executed each year.

Internet censorship

Internet censorship remains pervasive in China with few signs that the authorities are prepared to relax policies of surveillance and control.

Religious persecution

Unofficial religious groups—such as the Falun Gong spiritual movement—are banned as "subversive" and individual practitioners detained.

CHINA

Workers' rights

Trade unions are illegal.

Reeducation through labor

Critics of the government and members of banned religions can be sent to a labor camp for up to four years, without charge or trial.

Torture

Torture is widespread in the criminal justice system—common methods include electric shocks, beating, and sleep deprivation.

Human rights activists

People who take a stand are harassed and arrested, often on vague charges such as "possessing state secrets." They include lawyers, journalists, HIV activists, and trade unionists.

Taken from: Amnesty International, 2009.

In January 2007 Ministry of Health spokesman Mao Qunan reportedly acknowledged that the government harvested organs from executed prisoners. Adequate, timely medical care for prisoners remained a serious problem, despite official assurances that prisoners have the right to prompt medical treatment. . . .

Routine Arrests and Violations of Privacy

Authorities arrested persons on charges of revealing state secrets, subversion, and common crimes to suppress political dissent and social advocacy. Citizens also were detained and prosecuted under broad and ambiguous state secrets laws for, among other actions, disclosing information on criminal trials, meetings, and government activity. Information could retroactively be classified a state secret by the government.

During the year human rights activists, journalists, unregistered religious figures, and former political prisoners and their family members were among those targeted for arbitrary detention or arrest. . . .

The law states that the "freedom and privacy of correspondence of citizens are protected by law;" however, the authorities often did not respect the privacy of citizens in practice. Although the law requires warrants before law enforcement officials can search premises, this provision frequently was ignored; moreover, the Public Security Bureau (PSB) and prosecutors can issue search warrants on their own authority without judicial consent, review, or consideration. Cases of forced entry by police officers continued to be reported.

During the year authorities monitored telephone conversations, facsimile transmissions, e-mail, text messaging, and Internet communications. Authorities also opened and censored domestic and international mail. The security services routinely monitored and entered residences and offices to gain access to computers, telephones, and fax machines. All major hotels had a sizable internal security presence, and hotel guestrooms were sometimes bugged and searched for sensitive or proprietary materials. . . .

Not Free to Worship

The constitution and laws provide for freedom of religious belief and the freedom not to believe, although the constitution only protects religious activities defined as "normal." The government sought to restrict legal religious practice to government-sanctioned organizations and registered places of worship and to control the growth and scope of the activity of both registered and unregistered religious groups, including house churches. To be considered legal, religious groups must register with a government-affiliated patriotic religious association (PRA) associated with one of the five recognized religions: Buddhism, Taoism, Islam, Protestantism, and Catholicism. The PRAs supervised the activities of each of these religious groups and liaised with government religious affairs authorities charged with monitoring religious activity. The government tried to control and regulate religious groups, particularly unregistered groups, and repression and harassment of unregistered religious groups intensified in the run-up to the Olympics. Nonetheless, freedom to participate in religious activities continued to increase in many areas. Religious activity grew not only among the five main religions, but also among the Eastern Orthodox Church and folk religions. . . . The government continued to repress groups that it designated as "cults," which included several Christian groups and Falun Gong. . . .

EVALUATING THE AUTHORS' ARGUMENTS:

This viewpoint was published by a government source; the viewpoint before it was published in a newspaper. Which source do you think is more credible? Why? List at least three reasons.

Islam Grants Human Rights

Zaid Shakir

"Islam in America has historically been characterized by a strong advocacy of human rights and social justice issues."

In the following viewpoint Zaid Shakir discusses human rights under Islam and the role these rights have played in modern American history. Shakir points to the United Nations Universal Declaration of Human Rights as the starting point for a definition of human rights. He says two rights in particular—the right to life and the right to freedom of religion—have a basis in the Qur'an, the Muslim holy book, and have been practiced historically by Islamic civilizations. He explains that connections between Islam and human rights violations are a modern phenomenon, an outgrowth of the terrible events of September 11, 2001. But historically, Islam has been embraced by Americans (and by civil rights leaders such as Malcolm X) as a means of regaining their human rights in the face of the racial, social, and economic inequality. Shakir suggests human rights can be further promoted under Islam by recasting the Islamic discussion of human rights using the Universal Declaration of Human Rights as a basis, and by replacing general Islamic laws—which can be interpreted very broadly—with concrete legal

Zaid Shakir, "American Muslims and a Meaningful Human Rights Discourse in the Aftermath of September 11, 2001," *Cross Currents,* Winter 2003. Reproduced by permission.

language that makes clear how disadvantaged groups can receive human rights protection from Muslim societies.

Zaid Shakir teaches Arabic, Islamic law, history, and Islamic spirituality at the Zaytuna Institute in Berkeley, California.

AS YOU READ, CONSIDER THE FOLLOWING QUESTIONS:
1. What does the "ennoblement" of a human being mean, and what rights does it guarantee?
2. What movement was the Nation of Islam a part of, and who were key figures of this movement, according to Shakir?
3. What is the current problem with *Shari'ah* law, and how does Shakir propose to remedy this?

Defining Human Rights

. . . A review of the relevant literature reveals a wealth of definitions for human rights. Some of these definitions are quite brief, others quite elaborate. However, few of these definitions deviate far from the principles delineated by the Universal Declaration of Human Rights (UDHR), issued by the UN General Assembly in 1948. That landmark document emphasizes, among other things:

> The right to life, liberty, and security of person; the right to freedom of thought, speech, and communication of information and ideas; freedom of assembly and religion; the right to government through free elections; the right to free movement within the state and free exit from it; the right to asylum in another state; the right to nationality; freedom from arbitrary arrest and interference with the privacy of home and family; and the prohibition of slavery and torture.

This declaration was followed by the International Covenant on Economic, Social, and Cultural Rights (ICESCR) in 1966. In the same year, the International Covenant of Civil and Political Rights (ICCPR) was also drafted. These arrangements, collectively known as the International Bill of Human Rights, were reaffirmed in the Helsinki Accords of 1975, and buttressed by the threat of international sanctions against offending nations. When we examine these and other international agreements governing human rights, we find a closely related set of ideas, which collectively delineate a system of fundamental or inalienable, universally accepted rights.

These rights are not strictly political, as the UDHR mentions: "The right to work, to protection against unemployment, and to join trade unions; the right to a standard of living adequate for health and well-being; the right to education; and the right to rest and leisure." In summary, we can say that human rights are the inalienable social, economic and political rights, which accrue to human beings by virtue of their belonging to the human family.

Defining human rights from an Islamic perspective is a bit more problematic. The reason for this is that there is no exact equivalent for the English term, "human rights," in the traditional Islamic lexicon. The frequently used Arabic term, *al-Huquq al-Insaniyya*, is simply a literal Arabic translation for the modern term. However, our understanding of the modern term, when looked at from the abstract particulars which comprise its definition, gives us insight into what Islam says in this critical area. For example, if we consider the word "right" (*Haqq*), we find an array of concepts in Islam, which cover the range of rights mentioned in the UDHR.

If we begin with the right to life, Islam clearly and unequivocally guarantees that right. The Qur'an states, "Do not unjustly take the life which Allah has sanctified" (Qur'an 6:151). Similarly, in the context of discussing the consequences of the first murder in human history, "For that reason [Cain murdering Abel], we ordained for the Children of Israel that whoever kills a human being for other than murder, or spreading corruption on Earth, it is as if he has killed all of humanity. And whoever saves a life, it is as if he has saved all of humanity" (Qur'an 5:32).

It should be noted in this regard, as the first verse points out, Islam doesn't view humanity as a mere biological advancement of lower life forms. Were this the case, there would be little fundamental distinction between human and animal rights, other than those arising from the advancement and complexity of the human mind. However, Islam views human life as a biological reality, which has been sanctified by a special quality that has been instilled into the human being—the spirit (*Ruh*). The Qur'an relates, "then He fashioned him [the human being] and breathed into him of His spirit" (Qur'an 32:9).

It is interesting to note that this spiritual quality is shared by all human beings, and precedes our division into nations, tribes, and religious collectivities. An illustration of this unifying spiritual bond can be gained from considering a brief exchange, which occurred between the Prophet Muhammad (Peace and Blessings of Allah be upon him), and a group of his companions (May Allah be pleased with them). Once a funeral procession passed in front of the Prophet (Peace and Blessings of Allah be upon him) and a group of his companions. The Prophet (Peace and Blessings of Allah be upon him) reverently stood up. One of his companions mentioned that the deceased was a Jew, to which the Prophet (Peace and Blessings of Allah be upon him) responded, "Is he not a human soul?"

Possession of this shared spiritual quality is one of the ways our Creator has ennobled the human being. Allah says in this regard, "We have truly ennobled the human being. . ." (Qur'an 17:70). This ennoblement articulates itself in many different ways, all of which serve to highlight the ascendancy of the spiritual and intellectual faculties in man. It provides one of the basis for forbidding anything, which would belittle, debase, or demean the human being, and its implications extend far beyond the mere preservation of his life. It guarantees his rights before birth, by forbidding abortion, except in certain well-defined instances; and after death, it guarantees the right of the body to be properly washed, shrouded, and buried. It also forbids the intentional mutilation of a cadaver, even in times of war, and forbids insulting or verbally abusing the dead, even deceased non-Muslims. While these latter points may be deemed trivial to some, they help create a healthy attitude towards humanity, an attitude that must be present if acknowledged rights are to be actually extended to their possessors.

If we examine other critical areas identified by the UDHR for protection as inalienable rights, we can see that Islam presents a very positive framework for the safeguarding of those rights. In the controversial area of religious freedom, where Islam is identified by

> **FAST FACT**
>
> According to a 2009 report by the Pew Forum on Religion & Public Life, one in four people on the planet is a Muslim.

many in the West as a religion which was spread by forced conversion, we find that Islam has never advocated the forced acceptance of its creed, in fact, the Qur'an unequivocally rejects this idea, "Let there be no compulsion in [accepting] Religion, truth clearly distinguishes itself from error" (Qur'an 2:256). Allah further warns His Prophet (Peace and Blessings of Allah be upon Him) against forced conversions, "If your Lord had willed, everyone on Earth would have believed [in this message]; will you then compel people to believe?" (Qur'an 10:99).

In this context, every human being is free to participate in the unrestricted worship of his Lord. As for those who refuse to do so according to the standards established by Islam, they are free to worship as they please. During the Ottoman epoch, this freedom evolved into a sophisticated system of minority rights known as the Millet System. Bernard Lewis comments on that system:

> Surely, the Ottomans did not offer equal rights to their subjects—a meaningless anachronism in the context of that time and place. They did however offer a degree of tolerance without precedence or parallel in Christian Europe. Each community—the Ottoman term was *Millet*—was allowed the free practice of its religion. More remarkably, they had their own communal organizations, subject to the authority of their own religious chiefs, controlling their own education and social life, and enforcing their own laws, to the extent that they did not conflict with the basic laws of the Empire.

Similarly, positive Islamic positions can be found in the areas of personal liberties, within the parameters provided by the Islamic legal code. We will return to a brief discussion of those parameters, and their implications for an Islamic human rights regime. However, it isn't the purpose of this paper to engage in an exhaustive treatment of this particular subject.

Stating that, we don't propose that Islamic formulations in this regard are an exact replica of contemporary Western constitutional guarantees governing human rights policy. Muslims and non-Muslims alike, when examining the issue of human rights within an Islamic legal or philosophical framework, should realize that human rights regimes, as we know them, are a contemporary political phenomenon, which have no ancient parallel. However, we are prepared to defend the thesis that Islam has historically presented a framework for protecting basic human rights, and that it presents a system of jurisprudential principles that allow for the creation of a viable modern human rights regime, totally consistent with the letter and spirit of Islam. Having said that, we should note that an uncritical use of the Islamic framework of jurisprudential principles as the basis for the creation of a modern human rights regime, or a meaningful discourse around that regime fails, for reasons we will now examine.

The Inadequacy of Current Muslim Approaches to Discussing Human Rights

Current Muslim approaches to discussing human rights are inadequate for a number of reasons, in terms of their ability to serve as the basis for a meaningful discourse here in the West. First of all, they are all characterized by a Godcentric approach. We read, for example, in *Human Rights in Islam*, a pamphlet published by the World Assembly of Islamic Youth: "Since God is the absolute and the sole master of men and the universe, and since He has given each man human dignity and honor. . . ." and "Thus, all human beings are equal and form one universal community that is united in its submission and obedience to God." A similar pamphlet published by the Institute of Islamic Information and Education, states: "Every human being is thereby related to all others and all become one community of brotherhood in the honorable and pleasant servitude to the most compassionate Lord of the Universe." Such statements immediately frame the issue of human rights in terms unacceptable to a vast majority of Westerners. Most people here in the secular West would reject the idea of religious strictures and concepts serving as the basis for social or political programs or policies. Others reject the idea of God outright. Hence, by introducing a discourse predicated on the acceptance of the existence of God, and His exclusive right to order human life, Muslims immediately deny the discourse the common ground necessary for it to proceed with any meaning or logic. Although the two citations mentioned above are from brief pamphlets, which by nature tend to be general and lack any academic rigor, lengthier exposés of the subject are similarly flawed. Again, we emphasize that this criticism isn't intended to question the viability of the Islamic position, only its inadequacy as the starting point for a meaningful discourse here in the West.

The quotations cited above illustrate another inadequacy in the current Muslim human rights discourse, namely, its gaping generalities. These generalities, in many instances, gloss over nagging problems in Islamic societies, providing neither the acknowledgement of those problems, nor any meaningful framework for their resolution. Statements concerning a united humanity under God, while entertaining to the average Muslim, provide no clue as to what rights accrue to atheists, communists, secularists, or others who would reject the legitimacy of such a brotherhood.

Similarly, proclamations such as: "According to Islam, Allah is Sovereign. Human beings are His vicegerents. Since the state is not sovereign so [sic] the greatest factor against the implementation of Human Rights is waived. . ." totally ignore the fact that Muslim people live under the authority of nation-states, most of which totally ignore the "sovereignty" of God. These states generally grossly violate the basic human rights of their citizens. As their sovereignty isn't acknowledged by contemporary Islamic human rights formulations, there is no theoretical or practical basis for restraining their hegemony, a hegemony that leads to very real human rights abuses.

Another inadequacy of current Muslim human rights formulations, illustrated by the above quotations, is that they aren't seminal. Their gross generalities, meaningless rhetoric, and unrealistic theoretical formulations, fail to provide the basis for crafting meaningful policies, legal frameworks, or administrative regimes to insure a realistic chance of their implementation. The implications of this latter critique will be discussed later.

Many contemporary Muslim writers attempt to advance an alternative scheme of Islamic human rights based on a framework provided by the concept of the overarching objectives of the Divine Law (*Maqasid al-Shari'ah*). This scheme, which hinges on the fact that all Divine Law has been instituted to ultimately preserve and foster religion, life, intellect, the family, and wealth, provides an authentic

Islamic basis for identifying and defining basic human rights. For all of the promise this scheme provides, it cannot uncritically serve as the basis for a meaningful human rights discourse here in the West. The reason for this is that in its traditional formulation, it is a scheme that prioritizes the preservation of those rights exclusively associated with Islam and Muslims.

This prioritization leads to many rulings that would constitute fundamental human rights violations here in the West. For example, after elaborating the loftiness of the objectives of the Divine Law in Islam, Dr. Muhammad Zuhayli, following many classical scholars, such as Imam al-Ghazali, goes on to assert that Islam legislates killing the apostate, punishing the heretic, censoring one who abandons prayer, or refuses to pay the poor due, in order to protect the sanctity of religion. All of these strictures would be considered violations of the fundamental human rights of those being censored, in the Western scheme, as the violators' freedom of thought and religion would all be infringed on. Similarly problematic strictures exist in those measures that have been legislated to protect life, intellect, and the family.

Again, the point here isn't to propose that such sanctions aren't valid, or are void of any benefit, the point is that their implications would have to be thoroughly considered before classically articulated schemes dealing with the objectives and benefits of the Divine Law are advanced as a basis for a meaningful human rights discourse here in the West. We will return to this issue in the final part of this paper—God-willing.

The Relevance of Human Rights for Islam in America

Islam in America has historically been characterized by a strong advocacy of human rights and social justice issues. This is so because it has been associated with people who would be identified as ethnic minorities. The first significant Muslim population in this country, the enslaved believers of African origin, would certainly fit that description. The various Islamic movements, which arose amongst their descendants, appeared in a social and political context characterized by severe oppression. That socio-political context shaped the way Islam was understood by the people embracing it. It was a religion, in all its variant understandings, which was seen as a source of liberation, justice, and redemption. When the ethnic composition of the Muslim community began to change due to immigration in the 1970s, 1980s, and into the 1990s, the minority composition of the Muslim community remained. These newly arriving non-European immigrant Muslims were generally upwardly mobile, however, their brown and olive complexions, along with their accents, and the vestiges of their original cultures, served to reinforce the reality of their minority status. This fact, combined with the fact that the most religiously active among them were affiliated with Islamic movements in the Muslim world, movements whose agenda were dominated by strong human rights and social justice concerns, affected the nature of the Islamic call in this country, keeping human rights concerns to the fore.

Illustrative of this human rights imperative is the stated mission of the Ahmadiyya Movement when it began active propagation in America. Mufti Muhammad Sadiq, the first Ahmadi missionary to America, consciously called to a multicultural view of Islam, which challenged the entrenched racism prevalent in early twentieth-century American society. This message presented Islam as a just social force, capable of extending to the racial minorities of this country their full human rights. However, there were strong anti-white overtones of the Ahmadi message, shaped by Mufti Muhammad Sadiq's personal experience, and the widespread persecution of people of Indian descent (so-called Hindoos) in America, which dampened the broader appeal of the Ahmadi message. Those overtones were subsequently replaced by the overtly racist proclamations of the Nation of Islam, which declared whites to be devils. In the formulation of the Nation of Islam, Islam came to be viewed as a means for the restoration of the lost preeminence of the "Asiatic" Blackman. This restoration would be effected by a just religion, Islam, which addressed the social, economic and psychological vestiges of American race-based slavery. In other words, Islam was the agent that would grant the Muslims their usurped human rights.

The pivotal figure who was able to synthesize these various pronouncements into a tangible, well-defined human rights agenda was Malcolm X. By continuing to emphasize the failure of American society to effectively work to eliminate the vestiges of slavery, he was an implicit advocate of the justice-driven agenda of the Nation of Islam, even after departing from that movement. His brutal criticism of the racist nature of American society, which he often contrasted with the perceived racial harmony of Islam, highlighted by his famous letter from Mecca, in which he envisioned Islam as a possible cure for this country's inherent racism, was the continuation of the original multicultural message of the Ahmadiyya Movement. Finally, his evolving thinking on the true nature of the struggle of the African American people, and his situating that struggle in the context of the Third World human rights struggle, reflected the human rights imperative which figured so prominently in the call of Middle Eastern groups such as Egypt's Muslim Brotherhood, and the Indian Subcontinent's Jamaati Islami, groups which had a strong influence on the founders of this country's Muslim Students Asssociation (MSA) in 1963.

These various groupings, along with the Dar al-Islam Movement, the Islamic Party, and Sheikh Tawfiq's Mosque of Islamic Brotherhood, which would develop in many urban centers during the 1960s and 1970s as the purveyors of an emerging African American "Sunni" tradition, a tradition consolidated by the conversion of Malcolm X to the orthodox faith, represented in their various agendas the crystallization of the sort of human rights agenda which Malcolm was hammering out during the last phase of his life. These groups all saw Islam as the key to liberation from the stultifying weight of racial, social, and economic inequality in America.

The Iranian Revolution of 1979 further strengthened this human rights imperative. The revolution was presented by its advocates in America, who were quite influential at the time, as an uprising of the oppressed Muslim masses to secure their usurped rights from the Shah, an oppressive "Taghut." This message, conveyed strongly and forcefully through the call of the Muslim Students Association—Persian Speaking Group (MSA–PSG) was extremely influential in shaping the human rights imperative in American Islam, not only because of its direct influence, but also because of the vernacular of struggle it introduced into the conceptual universe of many American Muslims, and the way it shaped the message of contending "Sunni" groups. The combined influence of these forces worked to insure that human rights issues were prominent in the call of Islamic organizations and individuals prior to the tragic events of September 11, 2001.

Muslim Human Rights Discourse and the Challenge of September 11, 2001

The tragic events of September 11 present a clear challenge to the human rights/social justice imperative of Muslims in North America. The reasons for this are many and complex. The apocalyptic nature of the attacks of September 11, particularly the assault on and subsequent collapse of the World Trade Center towers, led many observers to question the humaneness of a religion that could encourage such senseless, barbaric slaughter. Islam, the religion identified as providing the motivation for those horrific attacks, was brought into the public spotlight as being, in the view of many of its harshest critics, an anti-intellectual, nihilistic, violent, chauvinistic atavism.

The atavistic nature of Islam, in their view, leads to its inability to realistically accommodate the basic elements of modern human rights philosophy. This inability was highlighted by the September 11 attacks in a number of ways. First of all, the massive and indiscriminant slaughter of civilians belied any Muslim claims that Islam respects the right to life. If so, how could so many innocent, unsuspecting souls be so wantonly sacrificed? Secondly, "Islam's" refusal to allow for the peaceful existence of even remote populations of "infidels," the faceless dehumanized "other," calls into question its respect for the rights of non-Muslims within its socio-political framework. It also highlights its inability to define that "other" in human terms.

As a link between the accused perpetrators of the attacks, Osama bin Laden and the Taliban rulers of Afghanistan, was developed by both the United States government and news media, the human rights position of Islam was called into further question. The Taliban, by any standards of assessment, presided over a regime that showed little consideration for the norms governing international human rights. Much evidence exists which implicates the Taliban in violating the basic rights of women, ethnic minorities (non-Pashtun), the Shi'ite religious minority, detainees, artists, and others, using in some instances, extremely draconian measures. Many of these violations occurred under the rubric of applying what the regime identified as Islamic law. The news of Taliban excesses, coupled with the shock of the events of September 11, combined to create tremendous appre-

Islamic women around the world march for equal rights. After the 9/11 terrorist attacks, the human rights position of Islam was called into question, including the treatment of women.

hension towards the ability and willingness of Islam to accommodate a meaningful human rights regime.

The political climate existing in America in the aftermath of September 11 has been exploited by certain elements in American society to call into question any humanitarian tendencies being associated with Islam. For example, in the aftermath of the brutal murder of Daniel Pearl, an act whose implications are as chilling as the attacks of September 11, Mr. Pearl's bosses at the *Wall Street Journal*, Peter Kahn and Paul Steiger, remarked, "His murder is an act of barbarism that makes a mockery of everything that Danny's kidnappers claimed to believe in." Responding to those comments, Leon Wieseltier, of *The New Republic*, stated, "The murder of Daniel Pearl did not make a mockery of what his slaughterers believe. It was the perfect expression, the inevitable consequence, of what his slaughterers believe." This, and similar indictments of Islam, challenge the ability of American Muslims to effectively speak on human rights issues in obvious ways.

If we examine the actual nature of American Muslim human rights discourse prior to September 11, we find that it was based in large part on Muslims contrasting the generalities of the *Shari'ah*, with the specific shortcomings of American society and history in relevant areas of domestic and international policy and practice. This discourse ignored the positive human rights strictures contained in sections of the American Constitution, the Bill of Rights, and the UDHR, to which the United States is a signatory. As in other areas, this inadequate approach produced a false sense of moral superiority among Muslims in America. This sense was shattered by the attacks of September 11, in that many Americans were suddenly pointing to what they viewed as the inadequacy of Islamic human rights regimes, their inadequate philosophical basis, and their failure to guarantee basic human rights protection, especially for women, religious, racial, and ethnic minorities living in Muslim lands.

Moving Ahead

Responding adequately to these charges will require a radical restructuring of current Islamic human rights discourse, and the regimes that discourse informs. The God-centric approach, which can serve as the basis for a strictly Islamic human rights discourse, cannot serve as the basis for such a discourse here in the West, at least in its initial phases. It lacks the necessary universality. Our efforts at such a discourse must be rooted in the UDHR. Although there are elements of the UDHR that we Muslims would object to, they are few, and as demonstrated above, most of the elements of the UDHR have legitimate Islamic parallels. Such an acceptance would not be illegitimate from an Islamic perspective, as virtually every Islamic nation is a signatory to the UDHR. Acceptance of the UDHR as the basis of our discourse, no matter how critical, would immediately give any Islamic discourse a universal base from which to proceed. It would also provide a framework to begin moving beyond generalities and into the realm of effective policy formulations and executive regimes.

Generalities, which formerly sufficed in Islamic human rights discourse will have to be replaced by concrete, developed policy prescriptions, which stipulate in well-defined, legal terms, how viable human rights protections will be extended to groups identified as systematically suffering from human rights abuses in Muslim realms.

An example of the dangerous and inadequate generalities alluded to above, can be glimpsed from a brief examination of the *Cairo Declaration on Human Rights in Islam* (CDHRI). Article 24 of that document states, "All the rights and freedoms stipulated in this Declaration are subject to the Islamic *Shari'ah*." Such a statement is meaningless, considering the vast corpus of subjectively understood literature that could be identified as informing the *Shari'ah*, unless the relevant rulings and principles of the *Shari'ah* are spelled out in exacting detail, and then effective executive regimes are created to guarantee those rights, once they are effectively enunciated. Existing executive regimes, such as that provided by the Helsinki Accords, can serve as viable models for Muslims, once the framework that led to those regimes has been accepted. This provides another incentive to root our discourse in the UDHR.

While this paper has consciously avoided mention of those features of Islam which would be antithetical to the Western concept of personal liberty, such as the lack of freedom to chose one's "sexual orientation," there are major civil liberties issues which must be addressed, in clear and unequivocal terms, if Islam's human rights discourse is to have any credence. Hiding behind Islam's cultural, or civilizational specificity to avoid providing answers to difficult questions will not advance a deeper understanding of our faith amongst enlightened circles in the West. Islam indeed has much to say in the area of human rights. However, much foundational work has to be done before we can speak clearly and authoritatively, especially in the changed post-September 11 political climate.

In *Islam and Human Rights*, Ann Elizabeth Mayer, whose work has been previously cited, acknowledges that

> the Islamic heritage comprises rationalist and humanistic currents and that it is replete with values that complement modern human rights such as concern for human welfare, justice, tolerance, and equalitarianism. These could provide the basis for constructing a viable synthesis of Islamic principles and international human rights. . . .

Our scholars have done much of the groundwork needed for a project such as the one alluded to by Mayer to move forward. For example, the Islamic concepts of *al-Aman*, and *al-Dhimmah*, concepts that provide the basis for protecting the lives and liberties of non-Muslims living in the Islamic realm, provide a viable framework for creating a modern regime capable of guaranteeing all of the rights ethnic and religious minorities enjoy in Western secular democracies. Similarly, the framework developed by scholars to discuss the overarching objectives of the Divine Law, despite the criticisms mentioned earlier in this paper, by examining the basic interests of the human being in a developed social context, and then categorizing those interests at the levels of essential needs, nonessential needs, and embellishments, provides an Islamic basis for legitimizing most of the fundamental rights identified by the UDHR.

Together, these and related Islamic concepts and frameworks provide the basic for an effective Islamic human rights regime. However, they will have to be further developed if they are to meet the challenges presented by Western ideas of rights and liberties, ideas shaped by the transformation of human thought and institutions by the ascendancy of secular humanism. Such development, far from being a betrayal of Islamic teachings, embodies their continued evolution. What we know as the institutions of the *Shari'ah*, in their classical sense, were the products of intellectual and institutional development commensurate to the level of societal advance existing in the days of their architects. In this day, when societies are far more complex and developed—both institutionally and intellectually—the *Shari'ah* must be developed to reflect that advance.

One of the great scholarly contributions of *Maqasid al-Shai'ah* was emphasizing the need to separate elements of legal thought from specific textual proofs. This process, an extension of the methodology of the *Mutakallimeen* scholars of jurisprudential principles, is essential if we Muslims are to generate the creative energy necessary to engage in grand projects. The restructuring of our thought on human rights and many other contemporary issues is such a project. Our rich heritage provides great insight into how we can proceed. If we are able to master that heritage, and use the best of it to address the burning issues of our day, we will be not only be able to engage in a meaningful discourse in the area of human rights, we will also be able to create a viable regime capable of transforming the best of our thought in this vital area, into meaningful policy prescriptions. Such an effort will not only enhance understanding Islam here in the West, it would also help us to begin correcting the pitiable human rights records of our Muslim states.

EVALUATING THE AUTHOR'S ARGUMENTS:

In this viewpoint Shakir presents a positive picture of Islam as a supporter of human rights and suggests that all cultures—even American culture—have been guilty of violating human rights at some point in their history. In your opinion, is this a valid claim? What kinds of human rights violations has the United States been guilty of over the course of its history? In your opinion, are these on par with human rights violations in Islam? Explain your reasoning.

Islam Violates Human Rights

Deborah Weiss

"*[The Islamic Human Rights Declaration] pits Muslims against non-Muslims and discriminates against women.*"

In the following viewpoint Deborah Weiss argues that Islam does not grant or respect human rights. She explains that dozens of Muslim countries have objected to the United Nations Declaration of Human Rights (UNDHR), the international human rights standard. Instead, they have submitted their own human rights document, one that Weiss says is weak on human rights. She criticizes it for granting men and women different, unequal rights and for saying Islam is superior to other religions. She also argues it grants the right to an *Islamic* education only and allows cruel, unusual, and unjust punishments. Weiss concludes that the rights granted by Islam are not rights at all and that people living in Muslim countries will not be free until their governments adopt universally accepted human rights.

Weiss is an attorney and senior fellow with the Center for Security Policy in Washington, D.C. Her articles have been published in the *Weekly Standard*, the *Washington Times*, and *American Thinker*. She is a survivor of the September 11, 2001, terrorist attacks on the World Trade Center in New York City.

Deborah Weiss, "Human Rights vs. Islamic Rights," *American Thinker,* December 11, 2008. Reproduced by permission.

AS YOU READ, CONSIDER THE FOLLOWING QUESTIONS:
  1. What is the UN Declaration of Human Rights (UNDHR), as described by Weiss?
  2. What rights does Weiss say are granted by the Universal Islamic Declaration of Human Rights?
  3. Why does the author say that the Cairo Declaration of Islamic Human Rights has a misleading title?

Yesterday [December 10, 2008] was the 60th Anniversary of the UN [United Nations] Declaration of Human Rights (UNDHR). The UN planned a big celebration, presenting seven awards to international figures who have made a mark in the human rights field this past year. One of the awards was posthumously earmarked to Benazir Bhutto, an advocate for true democracy in Pakistan assassinated during her campaign for Prime Minister.

Great strides have been made in the progress for human rights since the UNDHR was drafted. Yet, several Islamic countries, most notably the 57 member states of the Organization of Islamic Conference (OIC), object. Instead, they are promoting the Cairo Declaration of Islamic Human Rights for Muslim-majority countries. Two NGO's [nongovernmental organizations] have filed an appeal to the UN High Commissioner of Human Rights, arguing that the Cairo Declaration and the UNDHR clash. They have requested an official ruling.

The UNDHR came into existence after WWII. When the Nazi atrocities perpetrated upon the Jews came to light, the world community realized that the UN Charter was not sufficiently specific to protect human rights. In response, the UNDHR was adopted by the General Assembly of the UN on December 10, 1948. It consists of 30 articles which cover a broad range of rights including social, political, economic and religious. Though not legally binding, the UNDHR is considered a foundational document in international human rights law. It has inspired the development of 50 human rights instruments around the globe including international treaties, national constitutions, and regional human rights laws.

The bedrock beliefs embedded in the UNDHR are the inherent dignity and equality of all, as well as the right to liberty and the brotherhood of all humanity. The document omits any mention of specific religions, but presumes that all religions and cultures are equal. It promotes equality between men and women, and requires that the human rights of children be protected.

Islamic Countries Reject Human Rights

So, what's not to like? According to Saudi Arabia, Pakistan, Iran, Sudan, and the other countries comprising the OIC, the UNDHR fails to take into account the "cultural and religious context of Islamic countries." Indeed, in 1981, the Iranian Representative to the UN construed the UNDHR to be a "secular interpretation of a Judeo-Christian tradition which can't be implemented without trespassing on Islamic law." In June 2000, the OIC resolved to support the Cairo Declaration as an alternative.

So, what's the Cairo Declaration? The pre-cursor to the Cairo Declaration was the Universal Islamic Declaration of Human Rights, first proclaimed in the 1980's by the Islamic Council at the International Conference on the Prophet Mohammad and His Message. The document was rooted in the belief that Allah alone is the law giver and the source of all laws. It espoused that the State has an obligation to establish an Islamic order, and that all laws must be based on the Qu'ran and the Sunnah, as compiled by Muslim scholars, jurists, and representatives of various Islamic movements.

> **FAST FACT**
>
> In Muslim nations such as Afghanistan, Nigeria, the Sudan, and the United Arab Emirates, it is legal to sentence people to amputation and death by stoning.

Many of these ideas were finalized in the 1990 Cairo Declaration of Islamic Human Rights. 54 Muslim-majority countries signed the document that year. Many of these countries had abstained from the first vote on the UNDHR. The strategy of abstaining rather than voting in opposition to UNDHR, allowed these countries to uphold the false appearance of supporting human rights, while at the same time precluding a sufficient number of yes votes necessary for the UNDHR to pass.

How does Cairo stack up to the UNDHR? Cairo, unlike the UNDHR is anything but a religion-neutral document. On the contrary, it overtly asserts that Islam is superior over other religions, and that the Islamic ummah [community] is the "best nation." It cites the Muslim community's role in guiding "a humanity confused by competing trends and ideologies," and claims that Islam is the solution to man's "chronic problems of this materialistic civilization." It lists separate rights for men and women rather than advocating for general equality. It precludes the State from taking a life or perpetrating bodily harm *except as allowed by Sharia (Islamic law)*. It entitles everyone to a State-funded Islamic education even if they are not Muslim, but refuses to fund education in any other religion. Freedom of expression is restricted by Islamic interpretation, and blasphemy is forbidden. Most ominously, Articles 24 and 25 assert that all interpretations of the so-called rights stipulated in the Cairo Declaration, must be interpreted through the eyes of Sharia law. Sharia is cited as the sole source of reference allowable for explanation and clarification of all articles in the Declaration. Therefore, the entire document and all the rights and freedoms contained therein, are in fact, limited to those which are in accordance with the Islamic Sharia.

No Rights for Non-Muslims, Women, and Others

In short, the Cairo Declaration is a religious document. It is not the rights of the individual that are protected, but the best interest of the Islamic Ummah (community). It pits Muslims against non-Muslims and discriminates against women. It allows stoning for adultery, amputation for theft, and the death penalty for blasphemy. Its freedom of religion does not include the freedom to leave Islam, and the proselytizing of other religions or of atheism is strictly forbidden. Freedom of expression and freedom to obtain information cannot be of a nature that weakens the faith of the Islamic society. It is no coincidence that many of the enumerated "rights" are not rights at all, but are actually limitations on rights and freedoms. Therefore, the Cairo Declaration cannot reasonably be interpreted as a declaration of human rights. It is more accurately a statement of obligations which are required to submit to the will of Allah.

The Cairo Declaration of Islamic Human Rights holds a misleading title. By limiting the rights otherwise guaranteed by the UNDHR

Women in Lahore, Pakistan, protest honor killings. The author says that the Cairo Declaration perpetuates human rights violations against many sectors of Muslim society, including women.

and confining rights to those permitted by Sharia law, the Cairo Declaration undermines the very rights it purports to protect. In a world where radical Muslims are at war with Jews in Israel, Hindus in India, Christians in the Sudan and moderate Muslims in their own countries, the Secretary General of the OIC, Ekmeleddin Ihsanoglu, still insists that Islamophobia is one of the root causes of the world's violence and instability. Further, he claims that Israel is the world's main human rights oppressor.

People in Muslim Lands Are Not Free

The OIC diligently works to enforce oppressive measures in Muslim lands and expand Islamic supremacy around the globe. Yet, the OIC Secretary General still has the audacity to request that the 60th anniversary of the UNDHR be used to engage in dialogue with countries of "different viewpoints and religions" in an atmosphere of "mutual respect and tolerance." In other words, the OIC, arch enemy of human rights, is demanding tolerance for the intolerant, and respect for the disrespectful.

Muslim Nations Are Among the World's Least Free

The Middle East and North Africa—where most of the world's Muslim countries are located—have the highest percentage of countries ranked "not free" by Freedom House.

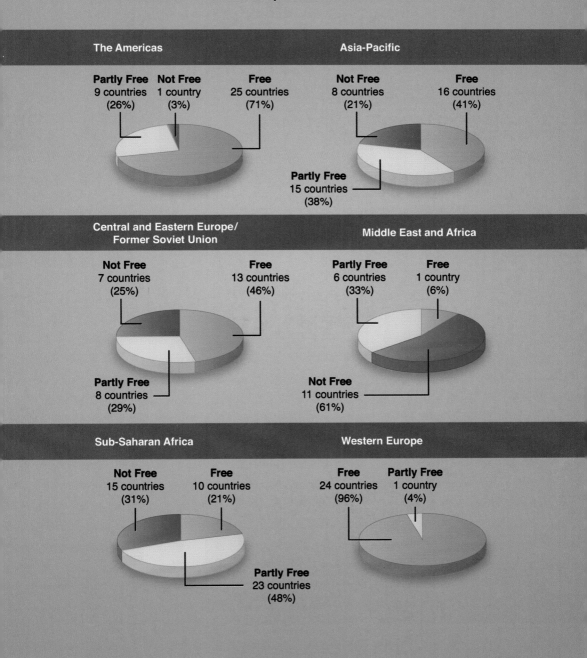

The Americas

Partly Free
9 countries
(26%)

Not Free
1 country
(3%)

Free
25 countries
(71%)

Asia-Pacific

Not Free
8 countries
(21%)

Free
16 countries
(41%)

Partly Free
15 countries
(38%)

**Central and Eastern Europe/
Former Soviet Union**

Not Free
7 countries
(25%)

Free
13 countries
(46%)

Partly Free
8 countries
(29%)

Middle East and Africa

Partly Free
6 countries
(33%)

Free
1 country
(6%)

Not Free
11 countries
(61%)

Sub-Saharan Africa

Not Free
15 countries
(31%)

Free
10 countries
(21%)

Partly Free
23 countries
(48%)

Western Europe

Free
24 countries
(96%)

Partly Free
1 country
(4%)

Taken from: Freedom House, 2009.

What is the reason that the OIC refuses to support the UNDHR? Does Islam conflict with fundamental human rights, basic freedoms and western values? Many moderate Muslims around the globe claim that it does not. But the leaders of the OIC insist that it does.

EVALUATING THE AUTHORS' ARGUMENTS:

In this viewpoint Weiss argues that Islam neither grants nor respects human rights. The author of the previous viewpoint, Zaid Shakir contends that Islam grants many human rights. After reading both viewpoints, with which author's perspective do you agree? Why?

Chapter 3

What Human Rights Policies Should the United States Follow?

A U.S. Soldier mans a guard post at Abu Ghraib prison in Iraq. The abuse of inmates at that prison by U.S. soldiers called America's commitment to human rights into question.

"The U.S. and other nations should stand with the people of Darfur and with African leaders from across the continent who are calling for an international peacekeeping force that can stop the violence and protect civilians."

The United States Should Commit Itself to Protecting Human Rights in Other Countries

Ann-Louise Colgan

Ann-Louise Colgan is the acting co-executive director of Africa Action, the oldest Africa advocacy organization in the United States. In the following viewpoint she argues that the United States has an obligation to protect and defend human rights in other countries. She makes her argument using the case of Darfur, an area in the Sudan that has been ravaged by war since 2003. Since the conflict began, 450,000 people have been killed, and 3 million have been displaced. Colgan says the United States should lead an international peacekeeping force to stop the atrocities being committed there. In her opinion U.S. resources, political clout, and military power put it in a strong position to take on the job

Ann-Louise Colgan, "Darfur: No More 'Never Again,'" TomPaine.com, October 11, 2006. Reproduced by permission.

of protecting human rights in weaker, smaller countries. She concludes that the United States must take action now before the humanitarian crisis in Darfur worsens.

AS YOU READ, CONSIDER THE FOLLOWING QUESTIONS:
1. What is UN Resolution 1706?
2. What is the "Responsibility to Protect" principle?
3. Who is H.E. Nana Effah-Apentang, and how does he factor into the author's argument?

As the crisis in Darfur[1] continues to deepen, the U.S. and other nations should stand with the people of Darfur and with African leaders from across the continent who are calling for an international peacekeeping force that can stop the violence and protect civilians in western Sudan.

A Human Rights Crisis

In recent weeks, reports have confirmed a sharp deterioration in the security situation on the ground in Darfur, and international discussions at the United Nations [U.N.], the African Union [AU] and elsewhere have focused on how to protect civilians from the worsening violence. While the AU continues to provide a measure of security in some parts of Darfur, and while it has extended the mandate of its mission until December 31 [2006], the need for a more robust international intervention in Darfur is clear. In a significant step, the U.N. Security Council authorized such a peacekeeping force in Resolution 1706—authorizing the deployment of U.N. peacekeeping troops—passed at the end of August.

> ### FAST FACT
>
> According to the *New Internationalist*, since the crisis in Darfur began in 2003, over 400,000 Darfurian civilians have died, and 90 percent of the villages of Darfur's targeted ethnic groups have been destroyed.

1. An area in western Sudan that has been ravaged by war, ethnic cleansing, rape, murder, and other atrocities since 2003.

We believe that Darfur is a real test for the international community of what is known as the "Responsibility to Protect" principle, affirmed by the United States and other nations just one year ago [2005]. As Mark Schneider of the International Crisis Group described it recently for TomPaine.com, the Responsibility to Protect doctrine was created so that "state sovereignty could not be used to justify atrocities—to bar collective international action to protect those citizens":

> [It] provides that diplomatic and other peaceful tools are tried first to bring the violations to an end, but where "national authorities manifestly fail to protect their populations from genocide, war crimes, ethnic cleansing and crimes against humanity," U.N. Security Council could put a Chapter VII military force on the table.

The United States Must Act to Protect Innocent People

The U.S. and other nations must act on their commitments to the Responsibility to Protect doctrine by implementing Resolution 1706. They must redouble their efforts to overcome any obstacles to its implementation. If [the capital of Sudan] Khartoum's consent cannot be achieved, they must find another way to implement the resolution and protect the people of Darfur. The Sudanese government's recent threats should not deter the international community.

With the implementation of Resolution 1706 now stalled in the face of Khartoum's opposition, African voices have emerged prominently in the discourse on Darfur, asserting the need and the obligation for new international action on this crisis. Leadership figures from across the continent have spoken out powerfully in the past several weeks, questioning the failure of the world community to act more quickly and assertively to save lives in Darfur. They have injected moral clarity into the debate and affirmed the legitimacy of the United Nations and its member states to pursue the action necessary to stop the genocide in Darfur.

It is important to elevate Darfuri voices in the U.S. discourse on this crisis. Africa Action [an advocacy organization] works with Darfuri organizations across the U.S., calling for an urgent international intervention that can provide protection and security to the people of Darfur. Fatima Haroun of the Sudan Peace Advocates

Americans Believe the United States Has a Responsibility to Protect Human Rights Worldwide

Do you think the United States has a responsibility to do something about the ethnic genocide in Darfur, or does the United States not have this responsibility?

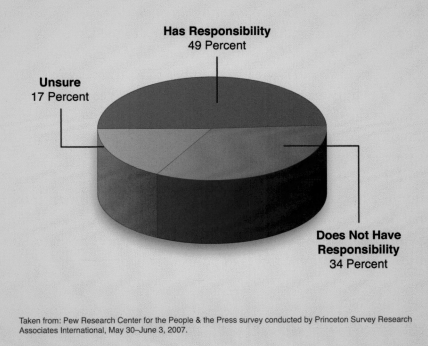

Has Responsibility
49 Percent

Unsure
17 Percent

Does Not Have Responsibility
34 Percent

Taken from: Pew Research Center for the People & the Press survey conducted by Princeton Survey Research Associates International, May 30–June 3, 2007.

Network joined Africa Action's rally outside the White House on September 9, 2006, and repeated her longstanding call for a United Nations peacekeeping force for Darfur. She emphasized: "The people of Darfur have suffered more than enough already, and the situation is getting worse. It is time for international action to stop the violence and bring relief and peace to this region."

The World Must Answer the Call to Protect Human Rights

The following week, on September 14, 2006, Archbishop Desmond Tutu emphasized, "The world can't keep saying 'Never again.'" He chastised the international community for its slow response to the Darfur crisis, saying in a BBC interview, "The harsh truth is that some lives are slightly more important than others. . . . If you are swarthy, of a darker hue, almost always you are going to end up at the bottom of the pile." Archbishop Tutu asserted that the international community should make clear to the Sudanese government that it must accept U.N. peacekeepers or face serious consequences.

At U.N. Security Council meeting on September 14, 2006, H.E. Nana Effah-Apenteng, Ambassador of Ghana to the United Nations, invoked Article 4 of the Constitutive Act of the African Union, which asserts the right to intervene in a member state in cases where crimes against humanity are taking place. He expressed his concern about the urgency of the situation in Darfur, and asserted that the international community could not allow Khartoum to delay action endlessly, but must move forward to protect the people of Darfur.

One day later, First Vice President in the Government of National Unity in Khartoum, Salva Kiir, offered his support for an international peacekeeping mission in Darfur, stating, "The aggravation of the humanitarian and security situation in Darfur necessitates intervention of international forces to protect civilians from the atrocities of the Janjaweed militias so long as the government is not capable of protecting them."

On September 17, [former] U.N. Secretary-General Kofi Annan told reporters, "I have urged the Security Council to act without delay, and to be united as possible in the face of the crisis." He added, "It is urgent to act now. Civilians are still being attacked and fleeing their villages as we speak."

Africa's first woman president, Liberian President Ellen Johnson-Sirleaf, addressed the General Assembly the following week on September 19, saying, "The world must not allow a second Rwanda to happen." She added, "My government therefore calls on this General Assembly and the Security Council to exercise the Chapter VII authority to restore peace, security and stability to Darfur."

The following day, Nobel Laureate Wole Soyinka was quoted in the South African newspaper *Business Day* challenging the legitimacy of Khartoum's opposition to a U.N. force for Darfur, saying:

When a deviant branch of that family of nations flouts, indeed revels in the abandonment of, the most basic norms of human decency, is there really justification in evoking the excuse that protocol requires the permission [for U.N. deployment of force] of that same arrogant and defiant entity?

The United States Must Lead Peacekeeping Efforts in Darfur

These and other statements from African leaders in the past month [September 2006] have shaped the debate on the necessary next steps to stop the genocide in Darfur. They join the chorus of voices from within and outside the continent urging an international intervention that can protect the people of Darfur.

The Abu Shouk refugee camp in Sudan houses over fifty thousand people. The author contends that the United States should protect the Sudanese from their own government's oppression.

The leadership role that the African Union has played and continues to play in Darfur is vital. The world should respect and heed the AU's numerous requests for a transition to a larger U.N. peacekeeping force. Such a transition is consistent with the international "Responsibility to Protect" doctrine, and it is the necessary and appropriate response to this crime against humanity.

The U.S. and other members of the Security Council must support African leadership on Darfur by implementing Resolution 1706 and deploying an international peacekeeping mission to reinforce the AU and provide effective protection to the people of Darfur. As the situation in Darfur deteriorates still further, the international community must act now. The Security Council must take every step necessary to overcome remaining obstacles and to achieve this deployment, before countless more lives are lost in Darfur.

EVALUATING THE AUTHOR'S ARGUMENTS:

Ann-Louise Colgan quotes from several sources to support the points she makes in her essay. Make a list of all the people she quotes, including their credentials and the nature of their comments. Then, analyze her sources—are they credible? Are they qualified to speak on this subject?

The United States Should Not Commit Itself to Protecting Human Rights in Other Countries

"Adopting a doctrine that compels the United States to act to prevent atrocities occurring in other countries would be risky and imprudent."

Steven Groves

In the following viewpoint Steven Groves argues that the United States cannot commit itself to defending human rights wherever they are violated. He explains that while the United States is committed to the spread and protection of human rights, many human rights violations occur in the world. If the United States were to commit itself to stopping all of them, it would quickly be bled dry of resources, personnel, money, and political authority. Groves believes America's first priority must be to itself; overextending itself in overseas conflicts threatens to make it vulnerable and

Steven Groves, "The U.S. Should Reject the U.N. 'Responsibility to Protect' Doctrine," *Backgrounder*, no. 2130, The Heritage Foundation, May 1, 2008, pp. 1–12. Reproduced by permission.

weak. For these reasons, Groves urges American policy makers to refrain from getting too involved in international humanitarian crises.

Groves is a fellow at the Margaret Thatcher Center for Freedom, a division of the Heritage Foundation.

AS YOU READ, CONSIDER THE FOLLOWING QUESTIONS:
1. What financial effect would protecting human rights in other countries have on the United States, according to Groves?
2. What did George Washington advise in his 1796 farewell address? How does this factor into the author's argument?
3. What does Groves say should not serve as America's barometer?

The "responsibility to protect" (R2P) doctrine outlines the conditions in which the international community is obligated to intervene in another country, militarily if necessary, to prevent genocide, ethnic cleansing, and other atrocities. Despite its noble goals, the United States should treat the R2P doctrine with extreme caution.

Adopting a doctrine that compels the United States to act to prevent atrocities occurring in other countries would be risky and imprudent. U.S. independence—hard won by the Founders and successive generations of Americans—would be compromised if the United States consented to be legally bound by the R2P doctrine. The United States needs to preserve its national sovereignty by maintaining a monopoly on the decision to deploy diplomatic pressure, economic sanctions, political coercion, and especially its military forces. . . .

If the United States intervenes in the affairs of another nation, that decision should be based on U.S. national interest, not on any other criteria such as those set forth by the R2P doctrine or any other international "test.". . .

Protecting Human Rights Worldwide Threatens the United States

If wholly accepted as official U.S. policy, the R2P doctrine would greatly expand U.S. obligations to prevent acts of genocide around the world. More important, adoption of R2P would effectively cede

American Priorities

Promoting and defending human rights in other nations is not a top priority for most Americans. Americans are more concerned with preventing terrorism, preventing the spread of nuclear weapons, and having access to a reliable energy supply.

"Which of the following should be a foreign policy priority of the United States?" (by percentage of respondents)

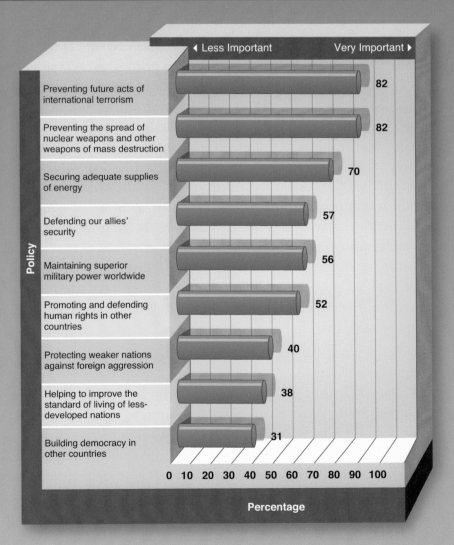

Taken from: Gallup Poll, February 7–10, 2005.

U.S. national sovereignty and decision-making power over key components of national security and foreign policy and subject them to the whims of the international community.

The U.S. government, as a party to the Convention on the Prevention and Punishment of the Crime of Genocide (the Genocide Convention), is currently obligated to prevent acts of genocide that occur within U.S. territory. . . .

However, adoption of the R2P norm would obligate the United States to prevent *all* acts of genocide, ethnic cleansing, and war crimes even if they occur outside of the U.S. Such an obligation would impose unique responsibilities. As the world's preeminent military force, the United States would have to bear a disproportionate share of the R2P international commitment. In the event that acts of genocide and ethnic cleansing occur, the vast majority of nations in the international community could reasonably plead military inferiority on each such occasion, leaving the United States to bear the brunt of any intervention. Most members of the international community could also plead poverty, again leaving the United States to fund the intervention. Even if the intervention is funded through the United Nations system, the United States would still pay an unequal share of the cost. . . .

The United States Must Protect Itself First

The United States must not surrender its independence and sovereignty cavalierly. The Founding Fathers and subsequent generations of Americans paid a high price to achieve America's sovereignty and secure the unalienable rights of U.S. citizens. The government formed by the Founders to safeguard American independence and protect individual rights derives its powers from the consent of the governed, not from any other nation or group of nations.

Having achieved its independence by fighting a costly war, America's Founders approached permanent alliances and foreign entanglements with a fair degree of skepticism. President George Washington, in his 1796 farewell address, favored extending America's commercial relations with other nations but warned against extensive political connections. Washington well understood that legitimate governments are formed only through gaining the consent of the people. He

President George Washington's 1796 farewell address warned against U.S. involvement in foreign affairs, advice that the author says should deter America from intervening in human rights issues in other countries.

therefore placed a high value on the independence that the United States had achieved and was rightfully dubious about involvement in European intrigues.

Integral to national sovereignty is the right to make authoritative decisions on foreign policy and national resources, particularly the use of the nation's military forces. Many of the reasons why America fought the War of Independence against Great Britain revolved around Britain's taxation of the American people without their consent and its practice of "declaring themselves invested with power to legislate for us in all cases whatsoever." Once America gained control of its revenue, natural resources, and industry and had formed a government separate and apart from any other, the Founders would not have compromised or delegated its prerogatives to any other nation or group of nations. Washington rightly warned his countrymen to "steer clear" of such foreign influence and instead to rely on "temporary alliances for extraordinary emergencies."

The United States Must Act in Its Own Best Interests

The R2P doctrine strikes at the heart of the Founders' notion of national sovereignty. The Founders would have deplored the idea that the United States would cede control—any control—of its armed forces to the caprice of the world community without the consent of the American people. Washington stated that the decision to go to war is a key element of national sovereignty that should be exercised at the discretion of the American government:

> Our detached and distant situation invites and enables us to pursue a different course. If we remain one people under an efficient government, the period is not far off . . . when we may choose peace or war, as our interest, guided by justice, shall counsel.

The U.S. interest, guided by justice and exercised with the consent of the American people, must remain the standard for making decisions of war and peace. The interest of the international community, which is guided by its own collective notion of justice and without the consent of the American people, should not serve as America's barometer, especially when placing the lives of U.S. military men and women in jeopardy. The United States cannot rely on world opinion, as expressed through an emerging international norm such as R2P, to set the proper criteria for the use of U.S. military force. The commitment to use force must be made exclusively by the U.S. government acting as an independent, sovereign nation based on its own criteria for military intervention.

In sum, the R2P doctrine does not harmonize with the first principles of the United States. Adopting a doctrine that binds the United States to scores of other nations and dictates how it must act to prevent atrocities is the very sort of foreign entanglement against which Washington warned us. The United States would betray the Founding Fathers' achievement of independence and sovereignty if it wholly acceded to the R2P doctrine.

EVALUATING THE AUTHORS' ARGUMENTS:

Authors Steven Groves and Ann-Louise Colgan disagree on whether the United States has a "responsibility to protect" human rights in other nations. What do you think? Does the United States have an obligation to defend human rights where they are violated, or does doing so threaten U.S. security and stability?

The United States Should Accept More Refugees from Iraq

"When Arabs castigate us for doing little for millions of refugees violently forced from Iraq, I must acknowledge that they are right. I nod in humility."

Justin Martin

The United States has an obligation to let in more Iraqi refugees, Justin Martin argues in the following viewpoint. He explains that the U.S.-led war in Iraq created millions of refugees who have nowhere to go. The United States has offered shelter to just a fraction of these people, while other nations—some of which had no involvement in the war—have let in many more. Since the United States started the war, Martin thinks it should be accommodating the greatest number of refugees. He concludes that the United States can let in many more Iraqis than it currently does and should make more of an effort to help these people rebuild their lives.

Martin has a PhD from the School of Journalism at the University of North Carolina, Chapel Hill.

Justin Martin, "Leaving Iraq's Refugees in the Lurch," *News & Observer* (North Carolina), February 14, 2009. Reproduced by permission.

AS YOU READ, CONSIDER THE FOLLOWING QUESTIONS:
  1. According to Martin, how many Iraqi refugees have surfaced since 2003? How many have been accepted into the United States?
  2. How many people does the author say were let into the United States from Russia and China in 2007?
  3. Who does the author describe as being "dusty and desperate"?

I've never been a self-hating American expatriate, although I've met a number of them in this part of the world [the Middle East]. I don't buy that my country is responsible for most, or even many, of the world's ills, and I'm filled with pride every Fourth of July and optimism every fourth November.

But I know that my country, like any other, has gotten some things wrong. And when one of these wrongs, the coldness the United States has shown Iraqi refugees, surfaces for discussion, I become visibly upset and deeply ashamed.

My country's claim of liberating Iraq means nothing without the liberation of those the campaign violently expelled from their country. The basic math is that around 2.2 million Iraqi refugees have been forced from their country since 2003, according to the United Nations [U.N.], and the United States has admitted just over 16,000, according to a *Baltimore Sun* report in December [2008]. This is about seven admitted refugees per 1,000.

The majority of the remaining 2 million–plus refugees are scraping by in Jordan, Syria and Lebanon, where the savings of many have been exhausted and unreplenished, since many can't find legal employment in these countries.

These numbers shame me to the core. Sweden has welcomed thousands more Iraqi refugees than we have.

The United States Can Do Much More

Think we can't absorb many more displaced Iraqis? According to Department of Homeland Security statistics, in 2007 alone the United States granted legal permanent residence status to 27,510

Refugees from Iraq arrive at a transit camp in Germany for processing. The author points out that the United States has taken in far fewer displaced Iraqis than other countries.

individuals from Vietnam, 41,593 from Russia, 70,924 from China, 25,441 from Cuba and nearly 900,000 more from over 180 countries.

I don't naively believe that we can admit anywhere close to 2 million Iraqi refugees, but based on these numbers, arguing we are doing all we can is indefensible.

Why the holdup on doing the right thing? Each year the U.S. officials conduct a relatively small number of costly and clogged interviews with Iraqi refugees hoping to move to the United States. While the number of annual interviews granted has recently increased, as has the number of refugees we pledge to admit each year, the numbers remain embarrassing. If, as promised, the United States admits 17,000 Iraqi refugees in fiscal year 2008–2009, the figure will be close to the number of Guatemalans to whom we give resident status every year.

Many Iraqi refugees wait for years in other countries to find out if the American dream is in fact just a dream. One such refugee is a young Iraqi woman whom I met in the quaint neighborhood of Jebel Amman. To protect her relatives' safety, she asked me not to use her name. In 1993, at age 7, residual unrest from the first Persian Gulf war forced her from Iraq to Jordan, where for nearly 16 years her relatives have been trying to get her to America. Year after year, America said no.

Finally, after another war has ravaged her native country, the U.N. has told her she will be relocated somewhere in Michigan. When, though, she does not know. "Maybe after another year," she told me.

This woman is among the luckier Iraqi refugees, for even though she's had to wait the better part of two decades for an American invitation, she's gotten her clearance and has most of her life in front of her. In Jordan, though, she will leave behind, hundreds of thousands of Iraqi refugees praying for similar fortune.

Iraqis Deserve More from America

While traveling in the Arab world, I hear many exaggerated claims about the evils of my government's foreign policies, and I sometimes chuckle at the crises blamed on the United States. I was once told by a Cairo cab driver that global warming would cease if only the United States would sign the Kyoto treaty [designed to cut global greenhouse gas emissions]—this he told me as our vehicle contributed to and cut through some of the most polluted air on Earth.

> # FAST FACT
>
> According to the Center for American Progress, as of 2008 the Swedish town of Sodertalje had resettled more Iraqi refugees than the United States as a whole.

But sometimes the criticism of my country is incisive and painful. When Arabs castigate us for doing little for millions of refugees violently forced from Iraq, I must acknowledge that they are right. I nod in humility.

I also reach for my pen, though, for citizens can still love and admire their nation with which they take issue, and that may make

Displaced Iraqis Around the World, 2007

The United States has taken in a tiny number of the people who have been displaced by the Iraq War.

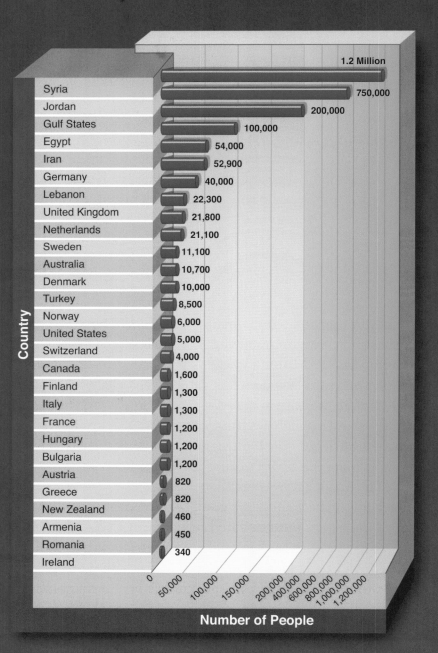

Taken from: Office of the UN High Commissioner for Refugees, 2007.

them even more determined to help their country inch back toward its better path. Just off our better path stand hundreds of thousands of exhausted refugees from Iraq, dusty and desperate and waiting for the liberation they were promised.

EVALUATING THE AUTHOR'S ARGUMENTS:

Justin Martin uses history, facts, and examples to make his argument that the United States should admit more refugees from Iraq. He does not, however, use any quotations to support his point. If you were to rewrite this article and insert quotations, what authorities might you quote? Where would you place these quotations to bolster the points Martin makes?

The United States Should Be Wary of Refugees It Accepts from Iraq

Todd Bensman

"The irony is that the war America started to make itself safer has forced more people regarded as security threats toward its borders."

In the following viewpoint Todd Bensman warns the United States to be careful of how many immigrants it lets in from Iraq because some of these people might be terrorists. He explains that although many of the 2 million Iraqi refugees are good people who just want to rebuild their lives, some may belong to one of the many radical Islamist movements afoot in Iraq. Bensman says these people could take advantage of their refugee status to gain entry into America and commit terrorist acts there. Or, says Bensman, terrorists from other Muslim countries might be able to enter the United States by pretending to be refugees from Iraq. For these reasons, Bensman suggests the number of Iraqi refugees let into the United States should be limited.

Bensman is an investigative projects reporter for the *San Antonio Express-News*, where this viewpoint was originally published.

AS YOU READ, CONSIDER THE FOLLOWING QUESTIONS:
1. Which U.S. state does the author say potential terrorists are sneaking into?
2. In what four countries does Bensman say the United States is battling radical Islamist movements?
3. Who is Steve Craw, and how does he factor into the author's argument?

Al Nawateer restaurant [in Damascus, Syria] is a place where dreams are bartered and secrets are kept.

Dining areas partitioned by thickets of crawling vines and knee-high concrete fountains offer privacy from informants and agents of the Mukhabarat secret police. The Mukhabarat try to monitor the hundreds of thousands of Iraq war refugees in this ancient city, where clandestine human smuggling rings have sprung up to help refugees move on—often to the United States.

But the refugees who frequent Al Nawateer, gathering around Table 75 or sitting alone in a corner, are undaunted, willing to risk everything to meet a smuggler. They come to be solicited by someone who, for the right price, will help them obtain visas from the sometimes bribery-greased consulates of nations adversarial or indifferent to American security concerns.

Some Immigrants Are Terrorists

The deals cut at places like Al Nawateer could affect you. Americans from San Antonio to Detroit might find themselves living among immigrants from Islamic countries who have come to America with darker pursuits than escaping war or starting a new life.

U.S.-bound illicit travel from Islamic countries, which started long before 9-11 [2001 terrorist attacks] and includes some reputed terrorists, has gained momentum and worried counterterrorism officials as smugglers exploit 2 million Iraq war refugees. The irony is that the war America started to make itself safer has forced more people regarded as security threats toward its borders.

A stark reminder of U.S. vulnerability at home came this month [May 2007] when six foreign-born Muslims, three of whom had entered the country illegally, were arrested and accused of plotting to attack the Army's Fort Dix in New Jersey. What might have happened there is sure to stoke the debate in Congress, which [in 2007 took] up border security and immigration reform. But the Iraqi refugee problem provides a twist on the question of what assurances America owes itself in uncertain times: What do we owe Iraqis thrown into chaos by the war?

Politically, immigration can be a faceless issue. But beyond the rhetoric, the lives of real people hang in the balance. A relatively small but politically significant number are from Islamic countries, raising the specter, some officials say, of terrorists at the gate. . . .

People from 43 so-called "countries of interest" in the Middle East, South Asia and North Africa are sneaking into the United States, many by way of Texas, forming a human pipeline that exists largely outside the public consciousness but that has worried counterterrorism authorities since 9-11. These immigrants are known as "special-interest aliens." When caught, they can be subjected to FBI interrogation, detention holds that can last for months and, in rare instances, federal prison terms.

The perceived danger is that they can evade being screened through terror-watch lists.

The Sources of Special-Interest Immigrants

The 43 countries of interest are singled out because terrorist groups operate there. Special-interest immigrants are coming all the time, from countries where U.S. military personnel are battling radical Islamist movements, such as Iraq, Afghanistan, Somalia and the Philippines. They come from countries where organized Islamic extremists have bombed U.S. interests, such as Kenya, Tanzania and Lebanon. They come from U.S.-designated state sponsors of terror, such as Iran, Syria and Sudan. And they come from Saudi Arabia, the nation that spawned most of the 9-11 hijackers.

Iraq war refugees, trapped in neighboring countries with no way out, are finding their way into the pipeline. Zigzagging wildly across the globe on their own or more often with well-paid smugglers, their disparate routes determined by the availability of bogus travel documents and relative laxity of customs-enforcement practices, special-interest immigrants often converge in Latin America. And, there, a northward flow begins.

Steve McCraw, director of the Texas Department of Homeland Security and a former assistant director of the FBI, said the nation's vulnerability from this human traffic is unassailable—even if not a single terrorist has ever been caught. "This isn't a partisan issue," McCraw said. "If the good guys can come, you know, then so can the bad guys. We are at risk."

Some Migrants Pose Serious Threats

Though most who cross America's borders are economic migrants, the government has labeled some terrorists. Their ranks include:

Mahmoud Kourani, convicted in Detroit as a leader of the terrorist group Hezbollah. Using a visa obtained by bribing a Mexican official in Beirut, the Lebanese national sneaked over the Mexican border in 2001 in the trunk of a car.

Nabel Al-Marahb, a reputed al-Qaida operative who was No. 27 on the FBI's most wanted terrorist list in the months after 9-11, crossed the Canadian border in the sleeper cab of a long-haul truck.

Farida Goolam Mahammed, a South African woman captured in 2004 as she carried into the McAllen [Texas] airport cash and clothes still wet from the Rio Grande. Though the government

In discussing threats posed by some immigrants, the author mentions the case of Farida Goolam Mahammed, a South African woman whose arrest led to the foiling of an attack on New York by al-Qaida.

characterized her merely as a border jumper, U.S. sources now say she was a smuggler who ferried people with terrorist connections. One report credits her arrest with spurring a major international terror investigation that stopped an al-Qaida attack on New York.

The government has accused other border jumpers of connections to outlawed terrorist organizations, some that help al-Qaida, including reputed members of the deadly Tamil Tigers caught in California after crossing the Mexican border in 2005 on their way to Canada. One U.S.-bound Pakistani apparently captured in Mexico drew such suspicion that he ended up in front of a military tribunal at Guantanamo Bay.

"They are not all economic migrants," said attorney Janice Kephart, who served as legal counsel for the 9-11 Commission and co-wrote its final staff report. "I do get frustrated when people who live in Washington or Illinois say we don't have any evidence that terrorists are coming across. But there is evidence."

According to U.S. Customs and Border Protection apprehension numbers, agents along both borders have caught more than 5,700 special-interest immigrants since 2001. But as many as 20,000 to 60,000 others are presumed to have slipped through, based on rule-of-thumb estimates typically used by homeland security agencies.

"You'd like to think at least you're catching one out of 10," McCraw said. "But that's not good in baseball and it's certainly not good in counterterrorism."

EVALUATING THE AUTHOR'S ARGUMENTS:

Todd Bensman raises the question of what Americans owe Iraqis whose lives have been destroyed by the U.S.-led war in Iraq. Given what you know, outline your position on this question, explaining what you think and why.

The United States Should Oppose the Use of Sweatshops

Rebecca Clarren

"Workers at RIFU and other Saipan garment factories labor six days a week, sometimes up to 20 hours a day."

In the following viewpoint excerpted from a much longer article, Rebecca Clarren explains that many clothes sold by America's most popular brands are made in sweatshops. The women who make them are like indentured servants, according to Clarren—they work six to seven days per week—sometimes for free—in unpleasant and abusive conditions. The author says that many of these sweatshops exist in U.S. territories, yet the U.S. government has taken little action to improve conditions for workers. Clarren thinks Americans should know that the cheap clothes they buy come at a high price—the exploitation and abuse of foreign workers.

Clarren is an investigative journalist based in Portland, Oregon, with a particular interest in labor issues. Her work has appeared in *Salon, Nation,* the *Los Angeles*

Rebecca Clarren, "Paradise Lost: Greed, Sex Slavery, Forced Abortions and Right-Wing Moralists," *Ms. Magazine,* Spring 2006.

Times Magazine, and *Ms. Magazine*, from which this viewpoint was taken. She has won five grants from the Fund for Investigative Journalism.

AS YOU READ, CONSIDER THE FOLLOWING QUESTIONS:
1. According to Clarren, how much do some garment workers pay to get a one-year job contract?
2. How long does Clarren say a worker who owes five thousand dollars to her employer must work for free to pay it off?
3. Why does Clarren consider some labels that say "Made in the USA" to be misleading?

*T*he whir of hundreds of sewing machines reverberates in the thick, dusty air at the RIFU garment factory. Inside this large warehouse, behind a guarded metal fence, 300 employees—most of them Chinese women—cut, sew, iron and fold blouses with such efficiency and focus that they seem like machinery themselves. From piles of orange and pink fabric, the workers will produce over 15,000 garments today for J. Jill, Elie Tahari and Ann Taylor. These name brand companies don't own the factory; like Liz Claiborne, The Gap, Ralph Lauren and others, they subcontract production to factories like this, scattered around the tiny Micronesian island of Saipan.

Counters above the sewing machines indicate how many pieces the women have completed. According to workers, if they can't finish a set quota of garments in a day, they may have to stay later and work for free, or they won't be eligible for future overtime opportunities—which they desperately need.

Coming from rural villages and the big city slums of poor Asian countries, these garment workers began their sojourn in the Marianas with a huge financial deficit, having paid recruiters as much as $7,000 to obtain a one-year contract job (renewable at the employer's discretion). Many of them borrow the money—a small fortune in China, where most are recruited—from lenders who charge as much as 20 percent interest.

Sweatshop Conditions Around the World

Many of the world's most popular brands use sweatshop labor to make their products.

UMBRO
A privately owned British company

Made in China

Workers are refused time off when ill. If workers leave the factory they lose a month's back pay.

MIZUNO
A privately owned Japanese company

Made in China

Workers are fined for flawed products. They are paid piece rates that vary according to how much work the management wants them to do.

PUMA
A privately owned German company

Made in Thailand

Women work double shifts and cannot refuse overtime because wages are so low.

ADIDAS
A privately owned German company

Made in Cambodia

Workers are required to work for long hours without breaks. Trips to the bathroom require their card to be stamped by a supervisor. During slow seasons their pay is so low it is hard to survive.

LOTTO
A privately owned Italian company

Made in Indonesia

Workers are humiliated and verbally abused on a daily basis. Women are subjected to sexual harassment by male supervisors and management.

FILA
A privately owned U.S. company

Made in Indonesia

Union workers are harassed by male supervisors and management.

Taken from: Oxfam and the Open University, 2004.

In a situation akin to indentured servitude, workers cannot earn back their recruitment fee and pay annual company supplied housing and food expenses of about $2,100 without working tremendous hours of overtime. Before being able to save her first dollar, a worker who owes, say, $5,000 to her recruiter has to work nearly 2,500 hours at Saipan's current minimum wage—which equals six more 40-hour workweeks than exist in a year.

And that's assuming she gets paid. Increasingly, workers are filing formal complaints that they have not received their wages, with some women going without paychecks for over five months. Still, workers at RIFU and other Saipan garment factories labor six days a week, sometimes up to 20 hours a day.

"One or two days a week we'd work through an entire night, and I was exhausted," says Chen Xiaoyan, 26, a nervous young woman with a thin ponytail who used to work for RIFU. "Sometimes we had no Sundays off either, but if you didn't want to work they'd allow you no overtime at all as a punishment."

The American consumers who wear the clothes these women produce probably have never heard of Saipan or the 13 other islands that comprise the Commonwealth of the Northern Mariana Islands (CNMI). Located just north of the U.S. territory of Guam, the islands were seized from the Japanese by U.S. military forces during World War II and served as the base for sending atomic bombs to Hiroshima and Nagasaki. After the war, the islands became a United Nations territory, administered by the United States.

Then, in 1975, the islands' indigenous population of subsistence farmers and fishermen voted to become a commonwealth

> # FAST FACT
>
> According to the anti-sweatshop organization DoSomething.com, a sweatshop worker's wages typically account for 1 to 1.5 percent of the final retail cost of a garment. For example, a worker is typically paid twenty-five cents to make a twenty-dollar shirt.

of the United States—a legal designation that made them U.S. citizens and subject to most U.S. laws. There were two critical exceptions, however: The U.S. agreed to exempt the islands from the minimum wage requirements of the Fair Labor Standards Act (allowing the islands to set their own lower minimum wage, currently $3.05, compared to $5.15 in the U.S.) and from most provisions of the Immigration and Nationality Act. This has allowed garment manufacturers to import thousands of foreign contract guest workers who, ironically, stitch onto the garments they make the labels "Made in Saipan (USA)," Made in Northern Marianas (USA)" or simply "Made in USA."

The USA label tells customers "the quality is really good," insists Cleofe de Guzman, a Filipina manager, as she walks down long, neat aisles past women pushing thin fabric through sewing machines. But to many Americans, adding USA to the label implies that goods are produced by Americans, not by foreign guest workers toiling under sweatshop conditions thousands of miles away.

The guest worker designation means that these foreign laborers can remain on the islands for an indefinite period but are not eligible for U.S. citizenship. If workers complain about conditions, not only can they be terminated at the whim of their employer, but because they're exempt from U.S. immigration law, they can be summarily deported.

The local Department of Labor and Immigration, chronically underfunded, is of little help to them, taking six months to a year to complete reviews of complaints. There are no labor unions. While there is a Federal Labor Ombudsman's office in Saipan, under the Department of the Interior's Office of Insular Affairs, it can do little more than offer translation services and refer aggrieved workers to other agencies; it has no authority to investigate or prosecute.

"There are serious problems here and everybody knows it," says the ombudsman, Jim Benedetto, as he stares out his Saipan office window at a sheet of rain. "There isn't anyone who would say there aren't worker abuses.". . .

A Myanmar migrant sews clothes for an American company in a Taiwanese-owned sweatshop in Thailand.

EVALUATING THE AUTHOR'S ARGUMENTS:

The author describes the conditions under which clothes from companies like the Gap, Ralph Lauren, J. Jill, and Liz Claiborne are made. Does knowing more about the production process of these clothes make you less likely to buy them? Why or why not?

The United States Should Not Oppose the Use of Sweatshops

Benjamin Powell

> *"What the third world so badly needs is more 'sweatshop jobs,' not fewer."*

Sweatshops are not necessarily bad for foreign workers, Benjamin Powell argues in the following viewpoint. He says that, on average, sweatshop workers earn more than other workers in their country. Even though their wages are low by American standards, Powell says that sweatshop workers earn more than twice what other workers in their country do. Furthermore, when sweatshops are closed, workers are often forced into worse occupations, such as prostitution. For these reasons, Powell concludes that the United States should not oppose the use of sweatshops to make products.

Powell is a senior economist with the Beacon Hill Institute and a professor of economics at Suffolk University in Boston.

AS YOU READ, CONSIDER THE FOLLOWING QUESTIONS:

1. What happened to fifty thousand children who were laid off from a sweatshop in Bangladesh, according to the author?

Benjamin Powell, "In Defense of 'Sweatshops,'" *Library of Economics and Liberty,* June 2, 2008. Reproduced by permission of the author.

I do not want to work in a third world "sweatshop." If you are reading this on a computer, chances are you don't either. Sweatshops have deplorable working conditions and extremely low pay—compared to the alternative employment available to me and probably you. That is why we choose not to work in sweatshops. All too often the fact that *we* have better alternatives leads first world activists to conclude that there must be better alternatives for third world workers too.

Sweatshop Jobs Are Better than Other Jobs

Economists across the political spectrum have pointed out that for many sweatshop workers the alternatives are much, much worse. In one famous 1993 case U.S. senator Tom Harkin proposed banning imports from countries that employed children in sweatshops. In response a factory in Bangladesh laid off 50,000 children. What was their next best alternative? According to the British charity Oxfam a large number of them became prostitutes.

The national media spotlight focused on sweatshops in 1996 after Charles Kernaghan, of the National Labor Committee, accused [Kathie] Lee Gifford of exploiting children in Honduran sweatshops. He flew a 15-year-old worker, Wendy Diaz, to the United States to meet [Kathie] Lee. [Kathie] Lee exploded into tears and apologized on the air, promising to pay higher wages.

> ## FAST FACT
>
> A 2008 study published by the Library of Economics and Liberty found that sweatshop wages tend to be two, three, and four or more times higher than the average national income in the country in which the sweatshop is located.

Should [Kathie] Lee have cried? Her Honduran workers earned 31 cents per hour. At 10 hours per day, which is not uncommon in a sweatshop, a worker would earn $3.10. Yet nearly a quarter of Hondurans earn less than $1 per day and nearly half earn less than $2 per day.

Wendy Diaz's message should have been, "Don't cry for me, [Kathie] Lee. Cry for the Hondurans not fortunate enough to work for you." Instead the U.S. media compared $3.10 per day to U.S. alternatives, not Honduran alternatives. But U.S. alternatives are irrelevant. No one is offering these workers green cards.

Economists have often pointed to anecdotal evidence that alternatives to sweatshops are much worse. But until David Skarbek and I published a study in the 2006 *Journal of Labor Research*, nobody had systematically quantified the alternatives. We searched U.S. popular news sources for claims of sweatshop exploitation in the third world and found 43 specific accusations or exploitation in 11 countries in Latin America and Asia. We found that sweatshop workers typically earn much more than the average in these countries. Here are the facts:

Anti-sweatshop activists hold a rally in New York City. The author argues that if such activists want the best for sweatshop workers, they would do well to support the improvement of sweatshops rather than demanding they be closed.

We obtained apparel industry hourly wage data for 10 of the countries accused of using sweatshop labor. We compared the apparel industry wages to average living standards in the country where the factories were located.

Sweatshop Workers Are Relatively Well Paid

Working in the apparel industry in any one of these countries results in earning more than the average income in that country. In half of the countries it results in earning more than three times the national average.

Next we investigated the specific sweatshop wages cited in U.S. news sources. We averaged the sweatshop wages reported in each of the 11 countries and again compared them to average living standards.

Even in specific cases where a company was allegedly exploiting sweatshop labor we found the jobs were usually better than average. In 9 of the 11 countries we surveyed, the average reported sweatshop wage, based on a 70-hour work week, equaled or exceeded average incomes. In Cambodia, Haiti, Nicaragua, and Honduras, the average wage paid by a firm accused of being a sweatshop is more than double the average income in that country. The [Kathie] Lee Gifford factory in Honduras was not an outlier—it was the norm.

Because sweatshops are better than the available alternatives, any reforms aimed at improving the lives of workers in sweatshops must not jeopardize the jobs that they already have. . . .

Evaluating Anti-Sweatshop Proposals

The anti-sweatshop movement consists of unions, student groups, politicians, celebrities, and religious groups. Each group has its own favored "cures" for sweatshop conditions. These groups claim that their proposals would help third world workers.

Some of these proposals would prohibit people in the United States from importing any goods made in sweatshops. What determines whether the good is made in a sweatshop is whether it is made in any way that violates labor standards. Such standards typically include minimum ages for employment, minimum wages, standards of occupational safety and health, and hours of work.

Such standards do nothing to make workers more productive. The upper bound of their compensation is unchanged. Such mandates risk

A Comparison of Sweatshop Workers' Wages

A study of sweatshop wages in ten countries found that in many of them, sweatshop workers earned two, three, four, or more times the average national income.

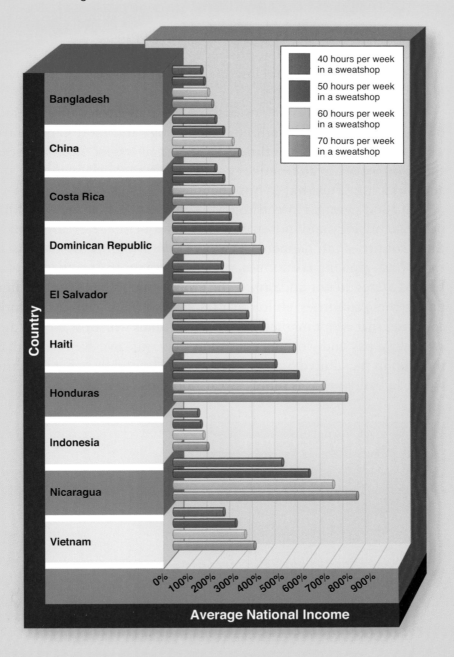

raising compensation above laborers' productivity and throwing them into worse alternatives by eliminating or reducing the U.S. demand for their products. Employers will meet health and safety mandates by either laying off workers or by improving health and safety while lowering wages against workers' wishes. In either case, the standards would make workers worse off. . . .

Not only are sweatshops better than current worker alternatives, but they are also part of the process of development that ultimately raises living standards. That process took about 150 years in Britain and the United States but closer to 30 years in Japan, South Korea, Hong Kong, and Taiwan.

When companies open sweatshops they bring technology and physical capital with them. Better technology and more capital raise worker productivity. Over time this raises their wages. As more sweatshops open, more alternatives are available to workers raising the amount a firm must bid to hire them.

The good news for sweatshop workers today is that the world has better technology and more capital than ever before. Development in these countries can happen even faster than it did in the East Asian tigers [fast-growing economies, such as Vietnam's]. If activists in the United States do not undermine the process of development by eliminating these countries' ability to attract sweatshops, then third world countries that adopt market friendly institutions will grow rapidly and sweatshop pay and working conditions will improve even faster than they did in the United States or East Asia. Meanwhile, what the third world so badly needs is more "sweatshop jobs," not fewer.

EVALUATING THE AUTHOR'S ARGUMENTS:

Powell argues that closing sweatshops hurts workers because they will be out of a job. What do you think? Do you think sweatshop jobs should be protected? What suggestions do you have for ways in which sweatshop conditions can be improved?

Facts About Human Rights

Editor's note: These facts can be used in reports or papers to reinforce or add credibility when making important points or claims.

Important Human Rights Documents

There are more than 150 international and regional treaties, declarations, conferences, or other documents that are dedicated to establishing and protecting human rights. These cover such topics as freedom of religion and speech; the right to happiness, marriage, property, income, and safety; women's rights; sexual orientation rights; children's rights; refugee and immigrant rights; and many more.

The Universal Declaration of Human Rights (UNDHR) is the most widely respected and cited human rights document. It was adopted in Paris by the United Nations General Assembly on December 10, 1948. It was approved by a vote of 48 to 0, with eight nations abstaining from the vote (Byelorussia, Czechoslovakia, Poland, Ukraine, the former Soviet Union, Yugoslavia, South Africa, and Saudi Arabia). It was adopted following the atrocities of World War II and was the first global expression of rights to which all human beings are entitled.

The UNDHR consists of thirty articles that grant a variety of rights. These articles include the following declarations:
- All human beings are born free and equal in dignity and rights.
- Everyone has the right to life, liberty, and security.
- No one shall be held in slavery or servitude.
- No one shall be subjected to torture or to cruel, inhuman, or degrading treatment or punishment.
- Everyone has the right to recognition everywhere as a person before the law.
- All are equal before the law and are entitled without any discrimination to equal protection of the law.
- No one shall be subjected to arbitrary arrest, detention, or exile.

- Everyone is entitled in full equality to a fair and public hearing by an independent and impartial tribunal.
- Everyone charged with a crime has the right to be presumed innocent until proved guilty.
- No one shall be subjected to arbitrary interference with his privacy, family, home, or correspondence, nor to attacks upon his honor and reputation.
- Everyone has the right to freedom of movement and residence within the borders of each state.
- Everyone has the right to leave any country, including his own, and to return to his country.
- Everyone has the right to seek and to enjoy in other countries asylum from persecution.
- Everyone has the right to a nationality.
- Men and women of full age have the right to marry and to found a family.
- Marriage shall be entered into only with the free and full consent of the intending spouses.
- The family is the natural and fundamental group unit of society and is entitled to protection by society and the State.
- Everyone has the right to own property alone as well as in association with others.
- No one shall be arbitrarily deprived of his property.
- Everyone has the right to freedom of thought, conscience, and religion; this right includes freedom to change his religion or belief, and freedom, either alone or in community with others and in public or private, to manifest his religion or belief in teaching, practice, worship, and observance.
- Everyone has the right to freedom of opinion and expression; this right includes freedom to hold opinions without interference and to seek, receive, and impart information and ideas through any media and regardless of frontiers.
- Everyone has the right to freedom of peaceful assembly and association.
- No one may be compelled to belong to an association.
- Everyone has the right to take part in the government of his country, directly or through freely chosen representatives.

- Everyone has the right of equal access to public service in his country.
- Everyone has the right to work, to free choice of employment, to just and favorable working conditions, and to protection against unemployment.
- Everyone, without any discrimination, has the right to equal pay for equal work.
- Everyone has the right to form and to join trade unions.
- Everyone has the right to rest and leisure, including reasonable limitation of working hours and periodic holidays with pay.
- Everyone has the right to a standard of living adequate for the health and well-being of himself and of his family, including food, clothing, housing and medical care, and necessary social services, and the right to security in the event of unemployment, sickness, disability, widowhood, and old age.
- Motherhood and childhood are entitled to special care and assistance. All children, whether born in or out of wedlock, shall enjoy the same social protection.
- Everyone has the right to education.
- Education shall be free, at least in the elementary and fundamental stages.
- Elementary education shall be compulsory.
- Higher education shall be equally accessible to all on the basis of merit.
- Education shall be directed to the full development of the human personality and to the strengthening of respect for human rights and fundamental freedoms.
- It shall promote understanding, tolerance, and friendship among all nations, racial, or religious groups, and shall further the activities of the United Nations for the maintenance of peace.
- Parents have a prior right to choose the kind of education that shall be given to their children.
- Everyone has the right freely to participate in the cultural life of the community, to enjoy the arts, and to share in scientific advancement and its benefits.
- Everyone has the right to the protection of the moral and material interests resulting from any scientific, literary, or artistic production of which he is the author.

The Status of Human Rights Around the World

According to Freedom House, an authoritative organization that ranks each of the 193 countries and 16 territories as "not free," "partly free," or "free":

The status of human rights improves every year:
- In 1978 the number of countries ranked free was 47; by 2008 that had grown to 89.
- In 1978 the number of countries ranked partly free was 56; by 2008 that had grown to 62.
- In 1978 the number of countries ranked not free was 55; by 2008 that had shrunk to 42.

In 2009 the majority of the world's countries were free:
- 42 percent were free (89 countries).
- 32 percent were partly free (62 countries).
- 22 percent were not free (42 countries).

However, more people lived in partly free or not free countries than in free ones:
- Citizens living in free countries: 3,055,885,000 (46 percent of the world's population)
- Citizens living in partly free countries: 1,351,014,000 (20 percent of the world's population)
- Citizens living in not free countries: 2,276,292,000 (34 percent of the world's population)

Of the 42 countries designated not free, eight countries and two territories received the survey's lowest possible ranking—"Worst of the Worst"—for political rights and civil liberties violations:
- North Korea
- Turkmenistan
- Uzbekistan
- Libya
- Sudan
- Burma

- Equatorial Guinea
- Somalia
- Tibet (territory)
- Chechnya (territory)

American Opinions About Human Rights

According to a 2009 Ipsos/McClatchy poll:
- 43 percent of Americans think the officials who authorized harsh interrogation techniques should be prosecuted.
- 48 percent do not.
- 30 percent think the soldiers who conducted the interrogations using harsh interrogation techniques should be prosecuted.
- 62 percent do not.

According to a 2009 CNN/Opinion Research Corporation poll:
- 50 percent of Americans approve of the George W. Bush administration's decision to authorize the use of harsh interrogation procedures, including waterboarding.
- 46 percent do not.
- Whether they approve of the techniques or not, 60 percent of Americans consider the techniques a form of torture.
- 57 percent do not think Bush administration officials who authorized the procedures should be prosecuted.

According to a 2009 CBS News/*New York Times* poll:
- 37 percent of Americans think using waterboarding and other aggressive interrogation tactics to get information from a suspected terrorist is justified.
- 46 percent say it is never justified.
- 71 percent consider waterboarding a form of torture.
- 62 percent say it is not necessary to investigate the Bush administration for misconduct.

An April 2009 Gallup Poll found that 55 percent of Americans believe it is justified to use harsh interrogation tactics to extract information from suspected terrorists.

Organizations to Contact

The editors have compiled the following list of organizations concerned with the issues debated in this book. The descriptions are derived from materials provided by the organizations. All have publications or information available for interested readers. The list was compiled on the date of publication of the present volume; the information provided here may change. Be aware that many organizations take several weeks or longer to respond to queries, so allow as much time as possible.

American Civil Liberties Union (ACLU)
125 Broad St., 18th Fl.
New York, NY 10004
(212) 549-2500
Web site: www.aclu.org

The ACLU is a national organization that works to defend Americans' civil rights guaranteed by the U.S. Constitution. The ACLU publishes and distributes policy statements, pamphlets, newsletters, and reports on various human and civil rights issues.

Amnesty International (AI)
322 Eighth Ave.
New York, NY 10001
(212) 807-8400
Web site: www.amnesty-usa.org

Amnesty International is a worldwide, independent voluntary movement that works to free people detained for their beliefs who have not used or advocated violence, and people imprisoned because of their ethnic origin, sex, language, national or social origin, economic status, and birth or other status. AI seeks to ensure fair and prompt trials for political prisoners and to abolish torture, "disappearances," cruel treatment of prisoners, and executions. Its Web site contains links to the numerous reports, brochures, and fact sheets it publishes.

Catholics for Choice (CFC)
1430 U St. NW, Ste. 301
Washington, DC 20009
(202) 986-6093
e-mail: cfc@catholicsforchoice.org
Web site: www.cath4choice.org

This organization promotes family planning to reduce the need for abortion and to increase women's choice in childbearing and child rearing. It publishes the bimonthly newsletter *Conscience.*

Child Labor Coalition (CLC)
1701 K St. NW, Ste. 1200
Washington, DC 20006
(202) 835-3323
Web site: www.stopchildlabor.org

The CLC serves as a national network for the exchange of information about child labor. It provides a forum for groups seeking to protect working minors and to end the exploitation of child labor. It works to influence public policy on child labor issues, to protect youths from hazardous work, and to advocate for better enforcement of child labor laws.

Family Research Council (FRC)
801 G St. NW
Washington, DC 20001
(202) 393-2100
e-mail: corrdept@frc.org
Web site: www.frc.org

The council is a research, resource, and education organization that promotes the traditional family and opposes condom distribution programs in schools. Among the council's numerous publications are the papers *Revolt of the Virgin, Abstinence: The New Sexual Revolution,* and *Abstinence Programs Show Promise in Reducing Sexual Activity and Pregnancy Among Teens.*

Global Exchange
2017 Mission St., Ste. 303
San Francisco, CA 94110
(800) 497-1994

e-mail: gx-info@globalexchange.org
Web site: www.globalexchange.org

Global Exchange is a nonprofit organization that promotes social justice, environmental sustainability, and grassroots activism on international human rights issues. Global Exchange produces various books, videos, and other educational programs and materials concerning human rights.

Human Rights First
333 Seventh Avenue, 13th Fl.
New York, NY 10001-5108
(212) 845-5200
Web site: www.humanrightsfirst.org

Human Rights First believes that building respect for human rights and the rule of law will help ensure the dignity to which every individual is entitled and will stem tyranny, extremism, intolerance, and violence. It advocate for change at the highest levels of national and international policy making.

Human Rights in China (HRIC)
350 Fifth Avenue, Ste. 3311
New York, NY 10118 USA
(212) 239-4495
e-mail: hrichina@hrichina.org
Web site: www.hrichina.org/public

Founded by Chinese students and scholars in March 1989, HRIC is an international, Chinese, nongovernmental organization whose mission is to promote international human rights and advance the institutional protection of these rights in the People's Republic of China. It publishes the quarterly journal *China Rights Forum*, and its Web site contains breaking news reports on events in China.

Human Rights Watch
350 Fifth Ave., 34th Fl.
New York, NY 10118-3299
(212) 290-4700

e-mail: hrwnyc@hrw.org
Web site: www.hrw.org

Human Rights Watch regularly investigates human rights abuses in over seventy countries around the world. It promotes civil liberties and defends freedom of thought, due process, and the equal protection of the law. Its goal is to hold governments accountable for human rights violations they commit against individuals because of their political, ethnic, or religious affiliations. It publishes the *Human Rights Watch Quarterly Newsletter*, the annual *Human Rights Watch World Report*, and a semiannual publications catalog.

International Campaign for Tibet (ICT)

1825 Jefferson Pl. NW
Washington, DC 20036
(202) 785-1515
e-mail: info@savetibet.org
Web site: www.savetibet.org

ICT is a nonpartisan, nonprofit organization dedicated to promoting human rights and democratic freedoms for the people of Tibet. It sponsors fact-finding missions to Tibet, works in conjunction with the UN and the U.S. Congress to protect Tibetan culture, and promotes educational and media coverage of human rights issues in Tibet.

International Labour Office (ILO)

1828 L St. NW
Washington, DC 20036
(202) 653-7652
Web site: www.ilo.org

The ILO works to promote basic human rights through improved working and living conditions by enhancing opportunities for those who are excluded from meaningful salaried employment. The ILO pioneered such landmarks of industrial society as the eight-hour workday, maternity protection, and workplace safety regulations. It runs the ILO Publications Bureau, which publishes various policy statements and background information on all aspects of employment.

National Endowment for Democracy (NED)
1101 Fifteenth St. NW, Ste. 700
Washington DC 20005
(202) 293-9072
fax: (202) 223-6042
e-mail: info@ned.org

The NED is a private, nonprofit organization created in 1983 to strengthen democratic institutions around the world through non-governmental efforts. It publishes the bimonthly periodical *Journal of Democracy.*

National Network for Immigrant and Refugee Rights (NNIRR)
310 Eighth St., Ste. 307
Oakland, CA 94607-4253
(510) 465-1984
e-mail: nnirr@nnirr.org
Web site: www.nnirr.org

This national organization is composed of local coalitions and immigrant, refugee, community, religious, civil rights, and labor organizations and activists. It serves as a forum to share information and analysis, to educate communities and the general public, and to develop and coordinate plans of action on important immigrant and refugee issues.

Planned Parenthood Federation of America (PPFA)
434 West Thirty-third St.
New York, NY 10011
(212) 541-7800
e-mail: communications@ppfa.org
Web site: www.plannedparenthood.org

The PPFA believes individuals have the right to control their own fertility without governmental interference. It promotes comprehensive sex education and provides contraceptive counseling and services through clinics across the United States. Its publications include the brochures *Guide to Birth Control: Seven Accepted Methods of Contraception* and *Teen Sex? It's Okay to Say No Way*, as well as the bimonthly newsletter *LinkLine.*

Youth for Human Rights International (YHRI)
1954 Hillhurst Ave., Ste. 416
Los Angeles, CA 90027
(323) 663-5799
e-mail: info@youthforhumanrights.org
Web site: www.youthforhumanrights.org

This independent nonprofit's purpose is to educate people about the Universal Declaration of Human Rights so they become valuable advocates for tolerance and peace. YHRI holds events and produces instructional tools to raise human rights awareness, such as the award-winning music video *UNITED*—a street-savvy, multi-ethnic, five-minute film in fifteen languages—conveying the power of human rights awareness. YHRI also publishes the *UNITED Human Rights Handbook*, which provides educators and leaders with a practical tool with which to teach human rights to the young.

For Further Reading

Books

Ching, Frank. *China: The Truth About Its Human Rights Record.* London, UK: Ebury, 2008. Examines the human rights situation in China, published to coincide with the 2008 Beijing Olympics.

Clapham, Andrew. *Human Rights: A Very Short Introduction.* New York: Oxford University Press, 2007. Takes an international perspective to focus on timely human rights issues such as torture, arbitrary detention, privacy, health, and discrimination.

Ishay, Micheline. *The History of Human Rights: From Ancient Times to the Globalization Era.* Berkeley and Los Angeles: University of California Press, 2008. Presents a spectrum of writers on human rights linked through time on themes such as the friction between individual and group rights and the rights of man versus the prerogatives of the state.

Rivoli, Pietra. *The Travels of a T-Shirt in the Global Economy: An Economist Examines the Markets, Power, and Politics of World Trade.* Hoboken, NJ: John Wiley & Sons, 2009. An economist interviews cotton farmers in Texas, factory workers in China, labor champions in the American South, and used-clothing vendors in Tanzania to expose the global production process of America's most popular products.

Timmerman, Kelsey. *Where Am I Wearing: A Global Tour to the Countries, Factories, and People That Make Our Clothes.* Hoboken, NJ: John Wiley & Sons, 2008. A journalist tracks a T-shirt, underwear, jeans, and flip-flops around the globe to see how and where they are made. An unexpected revelation is just how much harm is done to workers when overseas manufacturers are boycotted.

Wilson, Richard Ashby. *Human Rights in the "War on Terror."* Oxford: Cambridge University Press, 2005. Asks whether human rights since the 9/11 attacks and the "war on terror" are a luxury the United States can no longer afford, or must such rights always remain a fundamental part of democratic politics, in order to determine the boundary between individual freedom and government tyranny.

Periodicals and Internet Sources

Amnesty International USA. "Human Rights in China 2008," 2009. www.amnestyusa.org/annualreport.php?=ar&yr=2008&c=CHN.

Bard, Mitchell G. "Human Rights in Arab Countries," American-Israeli Cooperative Enterprise, 2009. www.jewishvirtuallibrary.org/jsource/myths/mf16.html.

Barnett, Don. "A New Era of Refugee Resettlement," Center for Immigration Studies, Backgrounder, December 2006. www.cis.org/articles/2006/back1006.pdf.

Batzell, Rudi. "Health Care as a Human Right," *Columbia Daily Spectator*, February 11, 2009. www.columbiaspectator.com/2009/02/10/health-care-human-right.

Byman, Daniel. "The Next Phase of the Iraq War: Why We Must Welcome Thousands of Iraqi Refugees to the United States," *Slate*, November 15, 2007. www.slate.com/id/2178065/pagenum/all/.

Carter, Jimmy. "U.S. Must Lead World on Human Rights," CNN.com, December 1, 2008. www.cnn.com/2008/POLITICS/12/01/jimmy.carter.rights/index.html.

Christianity Today. "China's Human Rights, In the Red," March 2009. www.christianitytoday.com/ct/2009/marchweb-only/110-52.0.html.

Cochrane, Kira. "An Abortion of Human Rights," *New Statesman*, October 23, 2006. www.newstatesman.com/200610230020.

Cohen, Roberta. "The Responsibility to Protect: Human Rights and Humanitarian Dimensions," Brookings Institution, February 20, 2009. www.brookings.edu/speeches/2009/0220_responsibility_to_protect_cohen.aspx.

Evans, Gareth. "Facing Up to Our Responsibilities," *Guardian* (UK), May 12, 2008. www.guardian.co.uk/commentisfree/2008/may/12/facinguptoourresponsibilities.

———. "The Responsibility to Protect: Holding the Line," OpenDemocracy.net, May 10, 2008. www.opendemocracy.net/article/the-responsibility-to-protect-holding-the-line-0.

Francis, Diane. "Time to Tap Canada's Water Riches: We Should Ignore Left-Wing Bleating and Exploit this Renewable Resource," *National Post* (Canada), September 27, 2006. www.nationalpost .com/story.html?id=dbb04244-e54d-48f7-bdbc-6d4d03383696.

Gleick, Peter H. "Human Right to Water," Pacific Institute, May 2007. www.pacinst.org/reports/human_right_may_07.pdf.

Gunther, Marc. "Is Water a Human Right?" *Huffington Post,* June 11, 2007. www.huffingtonpost.com/marc-gunther/is-water-a-human-right_b_51645.html.

Hoagland, Jim. "An African Crisis for Obama," *Washington Post,* November 16, 2008. www.washingtonpost.com/wp-dyn/content/article/2008/11/14/AR2008111403059.html.

Hoar, Joseph P. "Abandoned at the Border," *New York Times,* August 31, 2007. www.nytimes.com/2007/08/31/opinion/31hoar.html?_r=1&oref=slogin.

ImamWay.com. "Islam Grants Human Rights and Freedom," February 2005. www.imanway.com/site/en/islam29.htm.

IslamGuiden. "Human Rights in Islam," WAMY Series on Islam, no. 10. www.islamguiden.com/arkiv/human.pdf.

IslamicWeb.com. "Human Rights in Islam." www.islamicweb.com/begin/human_rights.htm.

Katulis, Brian, and Peter Juul. "The United States Can Do More for Iraqi Refugees," Center for American Progress, April 30, 2008. www.americanprogress.org/issues/2008/04/refugees_more.html.

Mineeia, Zainab. "U.S. Needs to Take In More Iraqi Refugees," AlterNet.org, October 10, 2008.

Pavone, Frank A. "Abortion: A Choice Against Women," Priests for Life. www.priestsforlife.org/brochures/abortionchoice.html.

Quinn, David. "Human Rights and Wrongs—Why Amnesty Abortion Belief a Mistake," *Independent* (London), August 17, 2007. www.independent.ie/opinion/human-rights-and-wrongs-why-amnesty-abortion-belief-a-mistake-1061204.html.

Redmond, Helen. "We Are Not Free: Health Care as a Human Right," Counterpunch.org, February 21, 2008. www.counterpunch .org/redmond02212008.html.

Richard, Anne C. "America's Responsibility to Iraqi Refugees," *Globalist*, October 31, 2007. www.globalpolicy.org/security/issues/iraq/attack/consequences/2007/1031usresponsibility.htm.

Valenzuela, Carmen Angélina. "Abortion Is a Basic Human Right," AlterNet.org, July 11, 2006. www.alternet.org/rights/38763/.

Watkins, Kevin. "Clean Water Is a Human Right," *International Herald Tribune* (New York), November 10, 2006. www.iht.com/articles/2006/11/10/opinion/edwatkins.php.

Younes, Kristele. "The Iraqi Refugee Crisis," *Foreign Policy in Focus*, March 14, 2007. www.fpif.org/fpiftxt/4059.

Yuging, Sun. "Human Rights Achievements Undeniable in China," *China Daily* (Beijing), November 12, 2008. www.chinadaily.com.cn/30znzw/2008-11/12/content_7197538.htm.

Zumwait, James. "Iran's 'Islamic Human Rights Day' Sham," *Human Events*, August 5, 2008. www.humanevents.com/article.php?id=27881.

Web Sites

Human Rights and the Drug War (www.hr95.org). This is the Web site of a multimedia project that documents in stories and photos the human rights consequences of the war on drugs.

Human Rights Education Associates (HREA) (www.hrea.org/index.php). HREA is an international nongovernmental organization that supports human rights learning, the training of activists and professionals, the development of educational materials and programming, and community-building through online technologies. Its Web site contains downloadable guides for teaching human rights.

Human Rights Library—University of Minnesota (www1.umn.edu/humanrts). This site, housed by the University of Minnesota, contains a large collection of international human rights treaties, instruments, general comments, recommendations, decisions, and other documents. It will be helpful to students researching primary human rights sources.

United Nations: Human Rights (www.un.org/en/rights). This page, sponsored by the United Nations, has fact sheets, news reports, and links about various human rights topics, including Darfur, child labor, Rwanda, children and armed conflict, and international human rights policies.

The Universal Declaration of Human Rights (www.un.org/en/ documents/udhr). This page contains the text of this renowned document, the human rights standard for most countries.

U.S. Department of State Human Rights Page (www.state.gov/g/ drl/rls.hrrpt). Contains links to the annual *Country Reports* published by the U.S. State Department, which contain authoritative information on the state of human rights around the world each year. Reports go back to 1999.

Index

violates human rights, 92–98
Islam and Human Rights (Mayer), 89

Picture Credits

Maury Aaseng, 16, 21, 26, 31, 36, 65, 73, 97, 103, 109, 118, 128, 137

AP Images, 87, 105, 116, 124, 135

ARIF Ali/AFP/Getty Images, 96

Michelle Del Guercio/Photo Researchers, Inc., 14

Antony Dickson/AFP/Getty Images, 11

Kevin Dietsch/UPI/Landov, 55

© Kevin Foy/Alamy, 29

David Gray/Reuters/Landov, 71

Ramzi Haidar/AFP/Getty Images, 38

Stan Honda/AFP/Getty Images, 99

Tony Karumba/AFP/Getty Images, 25

Toshifumi Kitamura/AFP/Getty Images, 45

Stefanos Kouratzis/AFP/Getty Images, 51

© Kader Meguedad/Alamy, 20

Chip Somodevilla/Getty Images, 42

Stock Montage/Hulton Archive/Getty Images, 111

Sukree Sukplang/Reuters/Landov, 131

Xinhua/Landov, 63